Controlling Our Children

Controlling Our Children

This book is part of the Peter Lang Education list.
Every volume is peer reviewed and meets
the highest quality standards for content and production.

PETER LANG
New York • Bern • Berlin
Brussels • Vienna • Oxford • Warsaw

Thomas David Knestrict

Controlling Our Children

Hegemony and Deconstructing the Positive Behavioral Intervention Support Model

PETER LANG
New York • Bern • Berlin
Brussels • Vienna • Oxford • Warsaw

Library of Congress Cataloging-in-Publication Data
Names: Knestrict, Thomas, author.
Title: Controlling our children: hegemony and deconstructing the positive
behavioral intervention support model / Thomas David Knestrict.
Description: New York: Peter Lang, 2019.
Includes bibliographical references and index.
Identifiers: LCCN 2018034360 | ISBN 978-1-4331-5560-4 (hardback: alk. paper)
ISBN 978-1-4331-5561-1 (ebook pdf) | ISBN 978-1-4331-5562-8 (epub)
ISBN 978-1-4331-5563-5 (mobi)
Subjects: LCSH: School psychology—United States.
Behavior Modification—United States.
School children—United States—Discipline.
Classroom management—United States.
School discipline—United States.
Classification: LCC LB1060.2 .K55 2019 | DDC 371.102/40973—dc23
LC record available at https://lccn.loc.gov/2018034360
DOI 10.3726/b13408

Bibliographic information published by **Die Deutsche Nationalbibliothek.**
Die Deutsche Nationalbibliothek lists this publication in the "Deutsche
Nationalbibliografie"; detailed bibliographic data are available
on the Internet at http://dnb.d-nb.de/.

The paper in this book meets the guidelines for permanence and durability
of the Committee on Production Guidelines for Book Longevity
of the Council of Library Resources.

Printed in Germany

Dedicated to my beautiful and brilliant best friend
and lifetime partner: Christine. I love you!

TABLE OF CONTENTS

ACKNOWLEDGMENTS

I would like to thank Mary Lisa Vertuca, Dr. Teresa Young, and Dr. Paul Gore of the Xavier School of Education for supporting me through my sabbatical to research and write this book. A special thank you to Dr. Laney Bender-Slack and Dr. Frank Fitch for their dedication and feedback in this project. Last, and certainly not least, the teachers, special educators, school psychologists, and students in the Cincinnati area schools that allowed me to witness these processes first hand.

PREFACE

Positive Behavioral Intervention Supports (PBIS) is a commonplace term these days in education. It is largely seen in a positive light and as something that works to the benefit of children. After all, it uses the word "positive." But it is the word "behavioral" that peaked my interest. As I investigated and deconstructed this framework and how it is implemented in the field I was disturbed by several facts. The first was that they chose the word "behavioral" for good reason. Most of what the research states as effective is behavioral in form and is premised on an "If, then" agreement. IF you do these things in this way, THEN you get this. That fact alone is a problem. Secondly, while typically school districts will front a very well-developed, three-tiered intervention system it is almost never used for children experiencing behavioral difficulties. Response to Intervention models for academically related interventions tended to follow the model fairly closely. However, even then intervention teams are very quick to pull the special education trigger. Doubly fast for behavioral issues. If one of the goals of intervention was to prevent special education identification, I did not see evidence of that. I also saw a dramatic discrepancy between what PBIS is stated to be in the research and what it actually is in practice. There seems to be an inevitable reduction to its lowest common denominator: simple bribes.

Lastly, and most disturbingly, I saw a tremendous discrepancy between the way districts dealt with poor and brown skinned children as compared to middle-class, affluent white children when it came to the issue of behavior and discipline in schools. This "disproportionality" is well researched, but there is little meaningful and contextually sensitive research completed when it comes to the efficacy of the very system that is sanctioned by districts, special education, and the federal government itself (Individuals With Disabilities Education Act [IDEA]). PBIS sounds innocuous and helpful. But is it? What was the history of its development and formation into a federally sanctioned framework? What are its origins and how does it manifest in schools today? Who does it benefit or harm? If it's not working why continue to use the model? A deconstruction of the system was called for.

This book represents the first steps in a protest movement. A microscopic look into systems that educators take for granted as positive forces for children. Breaking open biases that change the personal future for thousands of children every day. Dr. Pamela Taylor of Seattle University taught me a very simple model when considering the social justice of an issue. I try to answer these three questions:

1. *Is it just?*—Does everyone have access to the opportunities of a free and appropriate education?
2. *Is it right*—does it meet the expectations that society demands both morally and ethically?
3. **Does it Cause Harm?**—In the end is anyone hurt by the use of this model?

The PBIS system is intertwined with special education and our societies focus on fixing what it sees as broken. It is also heavily influenced by educators and politicians' obsessive need to measure all things. It is hard to see where one ends and the other begins. Finally, PBIS is both a product of and enmeshed with the continued faith and dependence on behaviorism and the usefulness of the carrot and the stick. It is time to understand why and develop a new, more responsive, and socially just framework of understanding. A model that helps develop autonomy, self-control, and self-reflection and helps in the development of individuals who will not be controlled by others.

INTRODUCTION

Five Core Problems

According to research the ubiquitous multilevel behavior intervention model known as Positive Behavioral Intervention Supports (PBIS) is said to have great potential to create different futures for many children. It is said that it has the potential to delay or prevent special education placement and labeling as well as offering a clearer and more direct route to behavioral support for students, allowing them to engage in academic instruction and in learning (Sugai & Simonsen, 2012). Sugai and Simonsen (2012) define "Positive Behavioral Intervention Supports (PBIS) as an implementation framework that is designed to enhance academic and social behavior outcomes for all students" (p. 1). However, the framework of PBIS is derived from a solidly behavioristic brain trust and continues to manifest itself as a system of glorified bribes to children to manipulate them into adopting behaviors, seen by the adults in power as desirable and appropriate. Likewise, these outcomes, guided by an obsession with obedience centered on white, middle-class, achievement-based values, largely developed independent of children's input, void of cultural sensitivity, and proven to not only be ineffective at helping children develop inner controls and autonomy but may also cause harm. Practice also suggests that PBIS is ironically most often used to hasten special education labeling and placement.

The discussion centering on behaviorism and constructivism is old and tired. One might ask why we are choosing to go down this road again. The pitfalls of behaviorism and the like have been well documented and well researched. However, these techniques are still widely used. Behaviorism and its various forms are still the primary modes of managing behavior in schools and are now sanctioned through Individuals With Disabilities Education Act (IDEA). This normalization of control by school districts, states, and the federal government should be examined and discussed.

The purpose of this book is to deconstruct the Positive Behavioral Intervention Support (PBIS) model and uncover the social injustice that is created by its use. The widely accepted framework for intervening upon behavior that is deemed chronic or inappropriate by the school authorities systematically uses methods that are based in behavioristic practices and have been shown to not only be ineffective but also create power relationships that segregate individuals emotionally, academically, and, sometimes, in the case of special education placement, physically. Deconstruction is part of the process of dialectical analysis. Furthermore,

> Dialectical analysis works on the basis of deconstructing a socio-historically specific entity, revealing its essential nature (as an oppressive process) and reconstructing an analytic account on the basis of revealed essence. The critical process that enables deconstruction and re-construction is dialectical shuttling between part and whole, abstract and concrete, past and present. (Royle, 2000, pp. 1–5)

To analyze any social justice issues that arise the Oakes, Lipton, Anderson, and Stillman (2015) framework will provide a social justice lens to analyze inequalities in the PBIS framework. This framework contains the following objectives targeted for analysis of PBIS practices:

1) To uncover, examine, and critique the values and the politics that undergird intervention practices and decisions
2) To challenge educational common sense (status quo) to ask important questions about why we do the things we do in school and who benefits from them
3) To attend to the ways in which behavioral interventions contribute to the creation, maintenance, and reproduction of inequalities, so we can construct more empowering alternatives and ways of thinking. Social justice is concerned with questions of power and decision-making. It also involves a consideration of the economic and cultural resources available to individuals and to particular communities and sectors within those communities. Throughout this book there

will be a reference at the beginning of each chapter listing the social justice-related points being addressed supported by the Oakes, Lipton, Anderson, and Stillman framework. Bell (2016) states that social justice is both a goal and a process. To break open social justice issues related to PBIS, it is necessary to deconstruct PBIS and then reconstruct a new, more socially just model:

> In accordance with the principles of equity, recognition, and inclusion. It involves eliminating the injustice created when differences are sorted, and ranked in a hierarchy that unequally confers power, social and economic advantages and institutional validity to social groups based their location in that hierarchy. (p. 4)

Bell (2016) argues that issues of social justice inevitably are issues of oppression. Oppression is the term used to describe the variables that create and sustain injustice and they are identifiable in the PBIS model (Bell, 2016). These issues are social constructions that have identifiable characteristics and will be used as a lens to view the injustices inherent in PBIS. They are:

1) *Restrictiveness*—PBIS has become institutionalized. It is ubiquitous. It also seeks to restrict and limit the influence of the student in the intervention on his/her behavior and is often heavily weighted in rewards and threats to encourage desired behaviors.
2) *Cumulative*—through the absorption of the culture the effects of PBIS and the oppression it engenders are cumulative over time.
3) *Durable and Mutating*—control-oriented behavior management has been denounced in the research. However, PBIS has mutated into a durable version of control and cultural dominance. While blatant racism is less obvious as in history, institutional racism and codes have mutated into the new racism. PBIS is simply a mutated version of control.
4) *Group-Based Categories*—PBIS places kids in categories that define them and sometimes last a lifetime.
5) *Hierarchical*—categories created by the PBIS process and the pseudo-scientific culture of special education create hierarchies identified as damaging. The dominant groups in school (white, middle-class leadership) hold the power and control, they determine how resources are allocated, and they define what is right and good (Bell, 2016).
6) *Hegemonic and Normalizing*—PBIS is coercive and creates hegemony. The process creates and maintains the hierarchy of "normal" and "abnormal" and couches these in pseudo-scientific language of special education and school psychology to create the illusion of "medicalized truth" (Foucault, 1963).

7) *Internalized*—when a practice is normalized people involved within its gaze learn to incorporate the oppression and beliefs into broader society. PBIS has broad acceptance by practitioners, students, and researchers alike even though there is evidence that it is an oppressive practice (Adams et al,2016).

8) *Intersecting*—The oppressive nature of PBIS intersects with other damaging phenomenon such as racism, sexism, and elitism to name three. Using these models to identify and break open the oppressive characteristics of the PBIS process and the often "life-defining" outcomes that can occur from traveling down this slippery slope is essential in identifying the damaging specifics of this model.

Five Core Problems With PBIS

Sloan-Cannella (1997) reminds us that we are all contextually grounded and are not discovering universal truths that should be imposed on all human beings; there are always regimes of truth. As such, there are shortcomings to the current universal PBIS model and the way it is consumed. Like water seeking its own level, behavioral interventions seem to be reduced to the lowest common denominator and formed into simple bribes for behaviors that are deemed appropriate by those in power. The unreflective nature of the behavioral perspective is problematic and manifests in the overrepresentation of underrepresented individuals as subjects of behavioral interventions. Fundamentally this approach creates a wide power differential between students and the adults designing and enforcing the interventions. This power differential constitutes a social justice problem. There are five core problems within the PBIS framework that serve as our focus in this book that will address all of these larger issues. These five concepts will be deconstructed and discussed using a social justice perspective that focuses on the power relationships created by a behavioral-based intervention model. Many in the field of education support a reconceptualization of much of American schooling. Sloan-Cannella (1997) wrote about reconceptualizing all of early childhood education. It is the purpose of this book to reconceptualize PBIS and uncover the social injustice that is just below the surface.

1) **The genealogy of PBIS and the fundamental theoretical flaws in the model**—When we peel back the genealogy of the PBIS model we find that it is of a behavioral lineage and is ensconced in a positivist

framework that values only observable behaviors as a reference. The internal workings that may or may not influence behavior choices are devalued in this model. This deep lineage continues to influence the research, development, and implementation of PBIS today. Outcomes of PBIS produce negative effects on many students, in particular, students from underrepresented groups. There is a disparaging power difference between students and the adults designing the interventions. This way of thinking about behavior supports the status quo through the explicit and implicit curriculums supported by PBIS (Beyer & Apple, 1988), creating a biased view of what is normal behavior, enforcing it, and creating reinforcement systems that support it. This is a vivid example of the banking curriculum (Freire, 1998).

2) *The problems that the* Applied Behavioral Analysis *(**ABA**)/positivist, behaviorist framework causes in creating a caustic and controlling environment that actually increases behavioral issues and decreases achievement and creativity*—Any behavioral approach will create an unequal power relationship. Freire (1998) wrote that teacher/student relationships are narrative in nature, with the teacher as the subject and the student a mere object or vessel to fill with facts. This "acting upon" is at the heart of a behavioristic philosophy—doing things "to" children to get them to behave the way we see as valuable as opposed to doing things "with" children to teach them ways to behave that work toward greater autonomy. The teacher is the person with power and the student must display the behaviors desired by the person in power in order to be rewarded. This is the embodiment of control. Likewise, there are concepts like the "Hedonic Adaptation" and "Fundamental Attribution Error" that make this approach untenable, whereas strategies that encourage a more intrinsic mindset and encourage the pursuit of optimal challenges are more innovative and tend to work better under challenging circumstances (Koestner, Zuckerman, & Koestner, 1987).

3) *Social Capital: Language, relationships, and autonomy are integral characteristics of strategies that assist individuals in changing behaviors the current model discourages*—Comer (2015) finds that what students need to develop is an inner locus of control and both intellectual and moral autonomy to attain social capital. The development of language and autonomy is dependent upon being able to learn and practice these skills working toward social capital

within a safe, nurturing, and supportive community with nurturing relationships. Currently, students are left out of the rule-making process. Freire (1990) spoke of this directly when he stated "… to alienate human beings from their own decision-making is to change them into objects" (p. 56). The objectification of students is a major flaw of this model and disproportionally affects underrepresented students. A socially just intervention system would rely on learning communities that are cooperative and allow members to learn from each other, reflect on their own experience, and make meaning of the larger systems and make meaning for themselves (Adams, Bell, & Griffin, 2016).

4) *How the Structure of Schools/Goals of School Curriculum prevent behavioral interventions from working for many students*—The structure of public schools, the social milieu, and the standardized, paced curriculum run counter to what we know is necessary to develop the social capital Comer talks about. These systems and structures also encourage expediency in managing behaviors, which an ABA, PBIS model provides. In addition, the tediousness of a true ABA behavior plan is not practical when you are teaching 30 children, 10 of whom might require a behavior plan. What ends up occurring is a devolved version of ABA that rests heavily on external control.

5) *The Contextual Shortcomings in the current model and how a new model will appropriately use research to guide practice*—With the identification of fundamental attribution error, there is an emphasis on fixing something in the child. Kohn (1999) states that it is not what we do "to" children that matters, it is what we do "with" them. Focusing almost entirely upon the child when developing intervention plans leaves out the possibility of the problem occurring outside of the child and quite possibly within the practice of the teacher. An intentional ecological approach to analyze these occurrences is needed. There is also a tendency of teachers to not want to look inward at their practice and the environment they have created. This defensiveness is derived from a low level of trust between teachers and administrators and is a function of the test-based culture. Students suffer because of this reality. The current model values the "product" of children behaving in the desired way and creating an obedient student body. Teachers involved during the writing of this book stated that they don't care what the child does anywhere else; he simply

needs to stop disrupting class and the learning of others. So they are drawn to simple bribes that garner them the "product" of a quiet and obedient child. While in the short term it seems like a positive outcome, in the long run we have taught the child that there is no value in being available for learning so we have to pay you to listen.

All five of these topics affect the attainment of a healthy, cooperative, and nurturing environment that is essential in teaching children how to internalize behavioral changes and manage themselves. What follows is a description of the PBIS model as it is currently configured.

Overview of the Current Model

PBIS has emerged as the accepted "best practice" for intervening upon individual's behavior (Sugai & Horner, 2002). The Individuals Disabilities Education Act (IDEA) specifies that Functional Behavioral Assessment (FBA) and PBIS are approaches that should be used to intervene on problematic behaviors prior to identification and can be used as ways to prevent identification or collect data toward identification. It has become the standard for prereferral intervention and was designed to prevent special education identification and placement but is in reality often used as a way to facilitate identification and placement and often results in marginalization of individuals (Ferri & Connor, 2005). It is also important to note that PBIS would not have come into existence were it not for the three-decades-long research history in ABA. The core values of PBIS originate from the values expressed within the ABA community (Alberto & Troutman, 2013). The intimate weaving of both ABA and PBIS remains strong today, and as a result, most PBIS are heavily influenced by behavioral concepts, strategies, and vocabulary. The arranging of consequences and Stimulus Response contingency, the concept of setting, events and stimulus control, generalization and maintenance of new behaviors remain bulwarks of PBIS today.

Proponents of PBIS have established journals, conferences, web pages in support of the practice (Brown, Anderson, & De Pry, 2015) and continue to support its use. While the practice is ubiquitous the actual outcomes are not as positive as the faith in the model would indicate. The fundamental basis for this model is based on a positivist framework that is oftentimes more concerned with sorting, controlling, or pathologizing students than with ameliorating behavioral issues (Woodley, 2004).

The use of PBIS in schools is widespread (Sugai & Horner, 2002). A basic tenet of the PBIS approach includes sorting all students into one of three categories based on risk for behavior problems. Once identified, students receive services in one of three categories: primary, secondary, or tertiary. To help practitioners with differences in interventions used at each of the levels the professional literature refers to a three-tiered (levels) model (Stewart, Benner, Martella, & Marchand-Martella, 2007; Sugai, Sprague, Horner, & Walker, 2000; Walker et al., 1996). Interventions are specifically developed for each of these levels with the goal of reducing the risk for the targeted behavior. The interventions become more focused and complex as one examines the strategies used at each level. As students are sorted to level two or three the nature of the interventions becomes more focused on the expediency of bribes for behaviors. "If you do this you will earn this" (Kohn, 1990).

Primary prevention strategies focus on interventions used on a school-wide basis for all students (Sugai & Horner, 2002). This level of prevention is considered "primary" because all students are exposed in the same way, and at the same level, to the intervention. The primary prevention level is the largest by number. Theoretically 80–85% of students react positively toward this level of intervention (Nelson, Martella, & Marchand-Martella, 2002). Primary prevention strategies allegedly include using effective teaching practices and curricula, explicitly teaching behavior that is acceptable within the school environment, focusing on ecological arrangement and systems within the school, consistent use of precorrection procedures, using active supervision of common areas, and creating reinforcement systems that are used on a school-wide basis (Lewis, Sugai, & Colvin, 1998; Martella & Nelson, 2003; Nelson et al., 2002). Primary supports would also include the development of cultural, school-wide norms and expectations as well as any externally controlled behavioral reward systems and consequences.

Secondary prevention strategies theoretically involve 15% of student's not responding to level one supports (Nelson et al., 2002). Interventions at the secondary level often are delivered in small groups to maximize time and effort and should be developed with the unique needs of the students within the group. Examples of these interventions include social support such as separate social skills training, *role-playing* or academic support (tutoring), or small group external reward systems and contracts. Additionally, secondary programs could include behavioral support approaches including Functional Behavioral Assessment or self-management training. These are interventions that are supposed to be developed collaboratively between the general education teacher, intervention specialist, and school psychologist or counselors. It is the first involvement of a specialist(s). Even with the heightened support within secondary level interventions some students will require a more individualized and/or intensive intervention (Walker et al., 1996).

Tertiary-level plans are also called intensive or individualized interventions and are the most comprehensive and complex. The purpose of these interventions is to reduce the intensity, the chronicity, or the frequency of behavior (Alberto & Troutman, 2013). The interventions within this level are strength-based in that the complexity and intensity of the intervention plans directly reflect the complexity and intensity of the behaviors. Students within the tertiary level continue involvement in primary and secondary intervention programs, if appropriate, and receive additional support as well (Lane, Kalberg, & Menzies, 2009).

Theoretically, if a child is shepherded through the three-tier PBIS model and there is no improvement in behavior measured, there should be enough data to warrant a multifactored evaluation or evaluation team report (ETR). This would be the initial evaluation for special education placement. Theoretically, a student must pass through this three-level intervention model, moving from less intense to more intense and targeted interventions prior to considering an ETR. In practice the reality is that schools rarely demand that students complete the circuit and rarely, if ever, is this system used to prevent special education identification. In fact it is often used to hasten special education identification and placement.

In practice PBIS has demonstrated, at best, mixed results for most students and even more questionable outcomes for children from underrepresented groups (Dishion, McCord, & Poulin, 1999). In deconstructing the process several inequities are found that serve to create the controlling relationships that many see as problematic (Knestrict, 2016; Pink, 2011). As a result, parents and students are often discouraged from participating meaningfully, classroom teachers feel inadequate and ineffectual while specialists typically dominate the intervention process from conception to fruition. The applied behavioristic framework for constructing an understanding of behavior dominates this perspective. This perspective often creates a hegemonic school culture (Kami, 1989), which encourages a reliance of external control and further encourages control of students instead of teaching them to change their behavior.

Within the Child

In the end the major paradigm shift in the discussion of revisioning PBIS is based on a fundamental understanding of how we develop autonomy and an internal locus of control with children. Is autonomy developed or assisted by rewards and punishment? Are these inner controls founded upon a hierarchical model of power and control? Is inner locus of control and self-discipline formed by doing things to children? Or doing things with children? Are these skills acquired by identifying a simple function for the behavior or by developing meaningful social relationships, within a safe and caring and challenging classroom environment that provides time and opportunity to practice and discuss these new skills within an environment stressing autonomy and self-control (Seligman, Ernst, Gillham, Reivich, & Linkins, 2009)

References

Adams, M., Bell, L. A., & Griffin, P. (Eds.). (2016). *Teaching for diversity and social justice: A sourcebook*. New York, NY: Routledge Press.

Alberto, P. A., & Troutman, A. C. (2013). Applied behavior analysis for teachers (9th ed.). Upper Saddle River, NJ: Prentice-Hall.

Beyer, L., & Apple, M., (1988). Values and politics in the curriculum. In L. Beyer & M. Apple (Eds.), The curriculum: Problems, politics and possibilities (pp. 334–350). Albany: SUNY.

Brown, F., Anderson, J., & De Pry, R. L. (Eds.). (2015). *Individual positive behavior supports: A standards-based guide to practices in school and community settings*. Baltimore, Maryland: Paul H. Brookes Publishing Company.

Comer, J. (2010). The Yale Child Study Center School Development Program. In J. Meece & J. Eccles (Eds.), *Handbook on schools, schooling, and human development* (pp. 419–433). New York, NY: Routledge.

Comer, J., & Ben-Avie, M. (2010). Promoting community in early childhood programs: A comparison of two programs. *Early Childhood Education Journal, 38*(2), 87–94.

Comer, J. P. (2015). Developing social capital in schools. *Society, 52*(3), 225–231.

Dishion, T. J., McCord, J., & Poulin, F. (1999). When interventions harm: Peer groups and problem behavior. *American Psychologist, 54*(9), 755.

Ferri, B. A., & Connor, D. J. (2005). Tools of exclusion: Race, disability, and (re) segregated education. *Teachers College Record, 107*(3), 453–474.

Foucault, M. (1963). *The birth of the clinic: An archaeology of medical perception* (A. M. Smith, Trans.). New York, NY: Vintage, 1975.

Freire, P. (1990). *Pedagogy of the oppressed*. New York, NY: Continuum.

Freire, P. (1998). *Pedagogy of freedom*. Lanham, MD: Rowman & Littlefield Publishers.

Kami, C. (1989). *Young children continue to reinvent arithmetic*. New York, NY: Teachers College Press.

Knestrict, T. (2016). The special education industrial complex. *Journal of Behavioral and Social Sciences, 3*(4), 201–211.

Koestner, R., Zuckerman, M., & Koestner, J. (1987). Praise, involvement, and intrinsic motivation. Journal of Personality and Social Psychology, 53, 383–390.

Kohn, A. (1999). *Punished by rewards: The trouble with gold stars, incentive plans, A's, praise, and other bribes*. Boston & New York: Houghton Mifflin Harcourt.

Lane, K. L., Kalberg, J. R., & Menzies, H. M. (2009). *Developing schoolwide programs to prevent and manage problem behaviors*. New York, NY: Guilford.

Lewis, T. J., Sugai, G., & Colvin, G. (1998). Reducing problem behavior through a school-wide system of effective behavioral support: Investigation of a school-wide social skills training program and contextual interventions. *School Psychology Review, 27,* 6–459.

Nelson, J. R., Martella, R. M., & Marchand-Martella, N. (2003). Maximizing student learning: The effects of a comprehensive school-based program for preventing problem behaviors. *Journal of Emotional & Behavioral Disorders, 10,* 136–148.

Oakes, J., Lipton, M., Anderson, L., & Stillman, J. (2015). *Teaching to change the world*. Boston: Routledge.

Pink, D. H. (2011). *Drive: The surprising truth about what motivates us*. New York: Penguin.

Royle, N. (2000) 'What is Deconstruction?', in N. Royle (ed.) Deconstructions: A User's Guide, pp. 1–13. Hamphire: Palgrave

Seligman, M. E. P., Ernst, R. M., Gillham, J., Reivich, K., & Linkins, M. (2009). Positive education. *Oxford Review of Education, 35,* 293–311.

Sloan-Cannella, G. (1997). *Deconstructing early childhood education: Social justice and revolution*. New York, NY: Peter Lang.

Stewart, R. M., Benner, G. J., Martella, R. C., & Marchand-Martella, N. E. (2007). Three-tier models of reading and behavior: A research review. *Journal of Positive Behavior Interventions, 9,* 239–253.

Sugai, G., & Horner, R. (2002). The evolution of discipline practices: School-wide positive behavior supports. *Child & Family Behavior Therapy, 24*(1–2), 23–50.

Sugai, G., & Simonsen, B. (2012). *Positive behavioral interventions and supports: History, defining features, and misconceptions*. Center for PBIS & Center for Positive Behavioral Interventions and Supports, University of Connecticut.

Sugai, G., Sprague, J. R., Horner, R. H., & Walker, H. M. (2000). Preventing school violence: The use of office discipline referrals to assess and monitor school-wide discipline interventions. *Journal of Emotional and Behavioral Disorders, 8,* 94–101.

Walker, H. M., Horner, R. H., Sugai, G., Bullis, M., Sprague, J. R., Bricker, D., & Kaufman, M. J. (1996). Integrated approaches to preventing antisocial behavior patterns among school-age children and youth. *Journal of Emotional and Behavioral Disorders, 4,* 193–256.

Woodley, A. (2004). Conceptualizing student dropout in part-time distance education: Pathologizing the normal? *Open Learning: The Journal of Open, Distance and e-Learning, 19*(1), 47–63.

· 1 ·

THE GENEALOGY OF POSITIVE
BEHAVIORAL SUPPORTS

Social Justice Points of Chapter One:

1. *Coercing and controlling others to fit "normal" is the status quo since PBIS inception.*
2. *The development of PBIS has had an obsession with fixing kids so they become "normal."*
3. *All of this history has been based on unequal relationships, which negatively impacts underrepresented kids more than others.*
4. *External control harms students and creates a junkie/dealer relationship.*
5. *PBIS amounts to a "banking education" model spoken of by Freire (1970).*
6. *PBIS is often seen as a way to hasten special education placement.*

The purpose of this chapter is to deconstruct the genealogy of the PBIS model to uncover the historical inequities evident in current practice. The deconstruction begins with an analysis of the genealogical underpinnings of the PBIS model. It results in the forming of several fundamental pillars of the model that serve as the foundation of PBIS practice today. The first is the historical evolution of the model deriving from behavioral psychology and a pathology-driven medical model and its pseudoscientific cousin, special education. The word "intervene" is defined as: "to involve oneself in a situation so as to alter or hinder an action or development" (American Heritage Dictionary, retrieved 5-11-2018). This implies someone or something taking action over another or a situation. Because the origins of this word are derived from a medical context, it often is still used with that context in mind. Children with chronic behavioral issues are in need of "intervention."

The second pillar uncovered in this deconstruction is the historical significance of behaviorism and its applied forms that support the evolution and development of the current model (Alberto & Troutman, 2012). PBIS is a derivative of Applied Behavior Analysis (ABA) and always has been intimately tied to the practice (Kincaid, Dunlap, Kern, Lane, Bambara, L., Brown, Knoster. 2016). When tracing the history and development of the PBIS model it is evident that the behavioristic worldview is prominent throughout. In the literature search for this chapter behavioral psychologist, school psychologist, and special education researchers conducted the majority of the research validating the use of PBIS and intervention. All trained largely in behavioral theory and practice.

The third pillar is the explicit and implicit curriculum that is created with the use of PBIS. The practice and implementation of this model has expected and unexpected outcomes as well as a hidden curriculum (Beyer & Apple, 1988). The intentional and expected outcomes are that of control and compliance in the name of academic achievement. The well-intentioned professional implementing PBIS would say that order is necessary for the effective instruction of others. However, with the control and obedience there are unexpected messages sent to the student being intervened upon, for example, the message sent when a bribe is used to encourage compliance, that is, "there is no inherent value in doing this behavior so we must pay you to do it." This implied message runs throughout all of PBIS and all of behaviorism in all its forms. Also, Freire (1970) described the "banking education" model of teaching. With this model he states that the student is the object and "empty vessel" that is filled only by the subject who is the teacher or authority implementing the behavior plan. It is implied that the authority has the knowledge and the power and is choosing to give it to the empty vessel of the student. The student has little to do with the development or implementation of the behavior plan imposed. The final pillar we will address in this chapter is the historical value placed upon the concept of normalcy and the mounting evidence that using this concept as a guiding principle has been and remains the single most damaging influence of the PBIS model. When PBIS is used the students are placed on the tier their behavior warrants. This is a judgment made by the teachers and professionals in the building. Almost never is the student or parent involved in placement or the development of the behavioral norms used to place students. Many see this as the first stage of the labeling process. It also has been identified as evidence that the PBIS model is simply a way of facilitating and eventually identifying students and placing them in special education.

Pillar One—The Genealogy of the Positive Behavioral Intervention Supports Model

The genealogy of PBIS follows a structure of change that is very similar to the evolution of prisons that Foucault (1979) describes. It begins with harsh public displays that often use physical punishment to control behavior but evolves to a more subdued, less physically punitive model. However, the goal of both the PBIS system and Foucault's idea of discipline and punishment is defining normal, coercing and controlling others to fit that description of normal (Foucault, 1977), usually ending with the segregation of the individuals. The genealogy of PBIS began in the early 1950s with the beginning of the Skinner dominance in psychology. There was an acceptance of European logical positivism, natural science models that overshadowed all other forms of interpretation in the so-called Western world (Morrow & Brown, 1994). Because of this faith in this "way of knowing," behaviorism and its progeny (behavior modification, ABA) became the only "science" worthy to observe and analyze human behavior. Watson (1958) stated that human beings should be studied in precisely the same way as you would analyze a chemical compound or the way a plant grows. Skinner believed that concepts like "freedom" and "self" were illusions (Skinner, 2014). The effect of patterning the study of human behavior after science leaves us with the reality that human beings are reduced to things and our motivations for behavior are reduced to reinforcements and avoidance of punishment (Kohn, 1999). These fundamental residues are still observable in the applied versions of behaviorism used in the PBIS model.

In the late 1960s there was a confluence of trends in the nation meeting together, eventually developing into what is now known as PBIS. There were several documentaries and newspaper article series addressing the treatment of individuals in hospital settings who were diagnosed with what was then called mental retardation. Chronic inappropriate behaviors were often dealt with by using aversive techniques such as hot sauce on the tongue, electric shock, restraints, or isolation. Films like "Christmas in Purgatory" (1966) and newspaper exposes on these circumstances led many to want to close these institutions and thus was born the deinstitutionalization movement. This was also a time in our country's history when there were significant strides made in civil rights issues, and the issue of deinstitutionalization became not only an ethical movement to end the abhorrent treatment of individuals with special needs, but also became, for the first time, a civil rights issue.

During the 1950s and 1960s, out of the field of special needs care and treatment sprung behavior modification. This set of techniques, born of B. F. Skinner's learning theory, was developing into the applied version of this method, which is referred to as "Applied Behavior Analysis" (Dunlap et al., 2009). The confluence of these historical trends met together to form a perfect environment for the development of a systematic, scientific framework, based in behavioristic research that could modify the behaviors of individuals with special needs.

There were several efforts in the 1980s to form frameworks to develop systematic technology to modify behavior, which included aversive techniques. Renzaglia and Bates (1983) wrote a textbook for teachers in training, which placed aversive techniques within a broader continuum from least intrusive to most intrusive. They theorized that aversive techniques might not be seen as appropriate by the layperson but were scientifically deemed appropriate within the right behavioral context. They also listed strategies of extinction, time out, verbal reprimands, restraint, overcorrection, and response cost as "more intrusive" but acceptable techniques in schools and institutions. Axelrod (1990) went as far as to say that techniques like electric shock and hot sauce were "quick fixes" to aberrant behaviors so that more appropriate behaviors could be taught in their place. It is interesting to note when reading the accounts of these times there was really no consideration of the ethical problems involved with using these methods by the behaviorists who developed them. Instead it was the perceived objections by the "laypeople" that prompted the examination.

Foucault (1977) wrote about a similar evolution of the genealogy of discipline and punishment when he wrote of the historical evolution moving from torture and a public display of punishment to a more private declaration of guilt and punishment that we see now with sentencing and incarceration. These techniques were seen as abhorrent to most school professionals and this rejection of aversive reinforcement by school professionals in particular led to new research to develop new technologies that (a) could address the same students, (b) would be socially appropriate and acceptable to laypeople and others in the community of practice, and (c) would be durable, efficient, and effective (Dunlap et al., 2009). During this time there was significant research and development of strategies that were nonaversive yet effective. Special education continued to be a major contributor to this research and this research in conjunction with behavioral psychology began to investigate the functionality of behavior. Asking the question "what purpose does this behavior serve? What function does it serve?" this early work by Donnellan, Mirenda, Mesaros, and Fassbender (1984) and Iwata, Dorsey, Slifer, Bauman, and Richman (1982) led to the technologies of functional analysis and functional assessment which now form a foundation of PBIS.

Gaylord-Ross (1980) developed a structured decision-making model that aided in the development of behavioral interventions and served as a foundation for the structured Intervention Assistance Model that was developed and improved by Zins, Curtis, Graden, and Ponti (1989) and Pugach and Johnson (1995). Meyer and Evans (1989) shifted the focus of this new technology to looking at the ecology and the antecedent events. Together they helped to create what eventually became known as "functional behavioral assessment," a variant analytic of ABA. Slowly, deliberately, a structure and framework was forming that facilitated analysis of behavior and testing of hypotheses, which encouraged a continuous improvement model for the development of interventions. As each intervention was tested adaptations were formed and a new version of the intervention was tried. This created a process by which a seemingly scientific method would improve treatment over time until the appropriate, effective, and durable intervention was arrived upon.

PBIS as We Know It Now

In 1987 the U.S. Department of Education provided funding research into nonaversive behavior management. Through these funds a training center was established that would research what they called the "technology of non aversive intervention supports." It was at this time that the faculty of this new research center coined the phrase "positive behavioral supports." In 1990 Horner et al. wrote a paper that defined the terms of this new technology that promoted "positive supports" and included the following characteristics of this new PBS model. They were:

1) Emphasis of Lifestyle Change
2) Functional Analysis

3) Multicomponent Interventions
4) Manipulation of Ecological Events
5) Emphasis of Antecedent Manipulations
6) Teaching Adaptive Behaviors
7) Effective Consequences
8) Minimizing Punishers
9) Distinguishing Emergency Procedures from Proactive Programming
10) Social Validation and the Role of Dignity of Behavioral Supports

Beginning with this article and buttressed by the support of the U.S. Department of Education the practice was legitimized and this framework was codified. This framework was written into a curriculum that was disseminated through a system of state training teams beginning in 1991 (Anderson, Albin, Mesaros, Dunlap, & Morelli-Robbins, 1993). During this time PBIS supports became increasingly recognized as a distinctive approach to the systematic control of chronic misbehavior in the classroom and in institutions. It was also thought at this time that it was crucial to create greater access to the ABA technology to teachers and laypeople working with individuals with difficult behavior.

The Multitiered Model

The final iteration of the PBIS model was the establishment of the multitiered model of intervention supports that was modeled after the trilevel triage medical model used in hospital settings (Merrell & Buchanan, 2006). As the PBIS model was implemented, it became obvious that the individual interventions were ineffective if the entire school culture was not addressed as a unit of analysis. Colvin, Kame'enui, and Sugai (1993) and Colvin, Sugai, and Kame'enui (1994) were the first to address the overall strategies used for the entire school. Tier one interventions were then conceived as a universal intervention for the entire milieu. This was also the point at which the School Wide Positive Behavioral Interventions and Supports (SWPBIS) model was used to sort students who were automatically placed within the model. If the external rewards were enough to prevent behavioral difficulties with a student and no "office discipline referrals" (ODRs) were issued then they would remain only under the influence of tier one supports. However, if students displayed escalating behaviors or an arbitrarily defined number of ODRs then tier two interventions would be developed and implemented. The nature of these tier two interventions would be increasingly restrictive and externally driven (Fairbanks, Sugai, Guardino, & Lathrop, 2007). Likewise, the most chronic and severely acting out students were placed within tier three and intensive; individualized interventions were developed and implemented. This research was still conceived within and adhered to the principles of ABA. By the late 1990s and early 2000s the multitiered SWPBS was fully developed and quickly became ubiquitous.

PBIS as Policy and Practice

The federal government sanctioned the use of the PBIS model in 2004 when the Individuals with Disabilities Education Act (IDEA) established PBIS and Response to Intervention (RTI) as available methods of intervention and identification. The terms RTI and PBIS are often used interchangeably. For the sake of this book the practice of RTI will refer to the systematic, tri level process used to develop interventions addressing academic issues while PBIS addresses behavioral issues. Both use a three-tiered model that places students on intervention levels ranging from the lowest (Universal Tier One), (Targeted Tier Two) and Intensive (Tier Three). Data gathered through these processes can be legitimately used for later identification in special education (Horner et al., 1990). Both of these also label students and place them on a level.

It was in the 1990s that the fundamental ideas of functional analysis, manipulation of ecological events, emphasis of antecedent manipulations, effective consequences and an effort to externally control the identified behaviors that were targeted for intervention. Likewise, it indicated the moment that the PBIS model would begin sorting and identifying students by the frequency and intensity of the behavior; a practice that is seen by many as the beginning of the special education identification and placement (Bornstein, 2017). Also, Bornstein (2017) identifies the PBIS model as encouraging the trading of a disciplinary system of control for a medicalized system of restoring order. PBIS is largely about comparing student behavior to the established norm. (2016) states that to understand disability you always have to return to the "normal body"; the problem is (often) not the student with the behavioral issue it rests with the way "normalcy" is constructed and forced upon the child. What is "normal" is determined by those in power. If a student can maintain themselves within the parameters of tier one expectations then they are considered "normal" by those in power. Behavior warranting tier two or three interventions are not. This facilitates the PBIS system's ability to sort students into normal and abnormal locations. Broderick and Leonardo (2016) used DisCrit theory to describe how school codes and rules institutionalize white behavioral norms as the accepted definition of "normal". Brantlinger (1997) illustrated this dynamic by stating that efforts to "fix" students who don't measure up to the established "white" version of normal determined by the tier one standards are classified and placed within more restrictive tiers of the PBIS system. She also identified the goal of PBIS as an effort to return all students to normalcy and to do so required a labeling and placement within the PBIS pyramid.

During the 1980s, a need was identified for improved selection, implementation, and documentation of effective behavioral interventions for students with behavior disorders (BD) (Gresham, 1991; Sugai & Horner, 1999; Walker et al., 1996). Because school psychology prefers to think of intervention development as a scientific proposition (Zins, Curtis, Graden, & Ponti, 1989) and because it is mandated as a "data driven" process (read quantitative) they rely almost completely on an ABA approach in observing children's behavior as well as developing interventions on their behavior (Evans, 1999). ABA is:

> A systematic application of behavioral principles to change socially significant behavior to a meaningful degree. Research tools enable users of these principles to verify a functional relation between behavior and intervention. (Alberto & Troutman, 2013, pp. 403)

This perspective of human behavior is logarithmic in nature and denies any heuristically derived information or insights. This is a specific perspective of human behavior that denies anything but observed behavior and affects the lens in which they view children. ABA requires that the behavior be targeted, observable and quantifiable (Dunlap et al., 2009). An outside manipulator is required to create the external controls necessary to motivate students to behave in a way that those in power deem as appropriate and desired. Often the context of the child's life is not taken into consideration when problem solving. Allegedly, the functional behavior assessment is supposed to determine the "function" or purpose of the student behavior. In essence asking the question "why is this student choosing this behavior. What are they getting from this"? This is a well-meaning effort to determine the reason the student chooses this behavior. Often the reasons for the behavior are hidden to both the student and the intervener. One professional related an analogy of student behavior that talked about chapters in the lives of children. She stated that often whatever occurred in the child's "chapter one" (earlier in the day, perhaps at home) affects or creates behaviors much later in the day in "chapter two". Sometimes we can't know what has occurred earlier with the child. Yet they are displaying this behavior in my class and the present time. In such cases interveners often only rely on the present and structure plans that are almost entirely based upon external variables or perceived "within child" deficiencies. Real change cannot happen without the student being an involved and active member in the effort to change the behavior. Children as young as 6 years old have been shown to be able to reflect on their behavior, become part of a larger community and value that experience enough to change their behavior without external control (Charney, 1998).

Historically, interventions have been closely related to special education. It is this fact that shows us that the construction of positive behavioral supports is inextricably linked to the idea that intervention is merely a stop along the way to special education identification and placement (Artiles, Harry, Reschly, & Chinn, 2002). Or a way to facilitate the identification process, pathologizing human behavior, moving from identifying "disorderly behavior" and medicalizing it to become "disordered behavior" (Bornstein, 2017). It is interesting to note that with the advent of PBIS the rates of identification of African Americans remains very high. With the ABA and RTI research touting success you would think there would be changes in these numbers (Harry & Klingner, 2014).

PBIS and Special Education

When tracing the genealogy of PBIS it is impossible to ignore the evidence that PBIS is an extension of the body of knowledge that created the separate silo called special education. Special Education is a social construction that some feel exists to maintain an unequal hierarchy that is sometimes referred to as the Special Education Industrial Complex (Knestrict, 2016). Knestrict (2016) uses a social justice framework to describe the development of behavioral interventions and the influence of the "logical positivist model underpinned by behaviorism" in the development of the model. Skrtic (1991) also found that

In the language of special education discourse, there is an assumption that disabilities are pathological conditions that students "have" virtually removing special education

> from the regular education discourse and segregating not only the discourse but also the teachers and students falling under the special education rubric. (p. 152)

In this pathology-based model it also becomes necessary to rely heavily on a logical positivist framework, which values empirical data and a logarithmic understanding of behavior, over theory and the more process oriented methods of changing and internalizing behaviors. Behaviorism, as with all positivist frameworks, assumes also that data are objective and self-evident. Foucault (1979) posited that this data are neither objective nor self-evident and they only serve to maintain the power structure of those in charge of the system. Because of the reliance on a pathological, logical positivist framework special education discourse became based in a medical model emphasizing defect and advocating diagnosis. This has elevated the practice to something more than it really is (Thomas & Loxley, 2001). These historical underpinnings create a process that is biased towards control of students, driven by faulty assumptions and steeped behavioristic ways of understanding the world and human behavior. Historically it creates and maintains a social and academic hierarchy keeping students of color down and creating a tiered system of academic achievement that is supported by the pseudo- legitimacy of special education (Bornstein, 2017). It also maintains the pathology based, medical model of dealing with behaviors in school rather than teaching new behaviors and emphasizing autonomy (Kohn, 1999).

Pillar Two—The Legacy of Behaviorism and ABA

Kohn (1999) writes in his response to behaviorism,

> There is a time to admire the grace and persuasive power of an influential idea, and there is a time to fear its hold over us. The time to worry is when the idea is so widely shared that we no longer even notice it, when it is so deeply rooted that it feels to us like common sense. At this point when objections are not answered anymore because they are no longer raised, we are not in control: we do not have the idea; it has us. (p. 3)

ABA is the applied version of behaviorism. While ABA is not behaviorism in a historical sense it still maintains the residue of the basic tenets of behaviorism. Mills (1998) in his analysis of the historical development of behaviorism presented several features that all behaviorists shared. He calls them "prior commitments." I believe that these "prior commitments" are present in the applied versions of behaviorism and affect the implementation of PBIS as a result. The first of these "commitments" is the belief and perceived value and effectiveness of the theory and it's applications. John Watson stated that he didn't care about the theory itself only that "the theoretical goal of psychology is the prediction and the control of behavior". This is evident in schools today when PBIS is used to control, identify, pathologize and place students not fitting into the behavioral rubric of a certain school (Bornstein, 2017). The second "prior commitment" is that they are suspicious and sometimes hostile to what they call "philosophical speculation". For example, a student may be being observed to have great behavioral difficulties in school. Acting out behaviors, verbal outbursts maybe even physical assaults. If all we are documenting and assessing are his outward behaviors we might never find out about the fact that his mom and dad were recently divorced and he is scared about his future. Such contextual realities should radically influence the type of intervention we use to support the child. However, if we are not looking we might miss this. Not valuing what behaviorists call "philosophical speculation" really means the devaluing of the contextual realities of human behavior many of which cannot be directly measured or seen unless there is a relationship with the child and he is able to share this information. This manifests in the belief that the inner workings of the mind are not as important as the observed behavior. It also manifest in the valuing of a more logarithmic view of human behavior that discounts or outright rejects a more heuristic view. The third "prior commitment" described is the acceptance of the pragmatic versions of positivism. Behaviorism, in all its forms, evolved from the positivist perspective (Mills, 1998). The Oxford Dictionary of Critical Theory defines logical positivism as:

> a school of philosophy informed by the principles of science and in doing so demonstrate the irrelevance of metaphysics. It applied a verification principle to all statements about the world and rejects all those that cannot be verified as true. (Retrieved 3-27-18)

In regards to PBIS/ABA a positivist view would look at external behavior as the only "knowable" data within a behavioral intervention. Thought process, and contextual information is not valued in the same way and there is often no effort to measure such a variable.

This idea reflects what Kohn (1999) views as a uniquely American sensibility. He states:

> It is no accident that behaviorism is this country's major contribution to the field of psychology, or that the only philosophical movement native to the United States is

pragmatism. We are a nation that prefers acting to thinking and practice to theory; we are suspicious of intellectuals, worshipful of technology, and fixed on the bottom line. We define ourselves by numbers- take home pay, cholesterol counts, percentiles, standardized test scores. By contrast we are uneasy with intangibles and unscientific abstractions such as a sense of well being or an intrinsic motivation to learn. (p. 10)

Thorndike, often called the "grandfather" of behaviorism was a positivist who saw the only reality is behavior that is observable and measureable (Thorndike, 1911). He stated, "if a thing exists it exists in some amount and if it exists in some amount then it can be measured" (p. 156). He also began to experiment with reinforcement in animals and observed what he called the "law of effect" stating:

Of several responses made to the same situation, those which are accompanied or closely followed by satisfaction to the animal will, all things being equal, be more firmly connected with the situation, so that when it recurs, they will likely recur; the greater the satisfaction or discomfort, the greater the strengthening or weakening of the bond. (p. 244)

The residue of behaviorism can be seen in the implementation of tier two and three interventions and the assessments used to measure the effectiveness of these interventions. This is evidenced by the use of Office Discipline Referrals (ODRs) as a unit of analysis in measuring the effectiveness of a given intervention. Historically they have used this single measure in much of the research that supports PBIS. There are two problems with this measure. The first is that ODR's are not always a valid indicator of an effective intervention or PBIS system and serve best as a single data point among many (Pas, Bradshaw, & Mitchell, 2011). But since ODR's are observable and measureable they are the preferred unit of analysis. The second issue with ODR's is that there are far more viable ways of measuring the effect of an intervention. Some have suggested that measuring engagement in the classroom should serve as a more valid unit of analysis. Take for example a situation where the intervention implemented decreased the number of ODR's but the teacher reports that the student's behavior, while not disruptive enough to warrant removal or an ODR, does warrant multiple time outs in the classroom, failure to complete tasks and a total lack of engagement in instruction. If the unit of measurement is limited to only ODR's we miss much of the qualitative and contextual information needed to design and implement an effective intervention plan. Measuring engagement is not as easy to do and requires interpretation. This type of assessment is often seen as a violation of the "prior commitment" of "philosophical speculation" and therefore invalid. ODR's fit the description of Thorndike's, they exist, they take up space, and they can be measured and can be used in a pre and post intervention assessment that will give you a quick and easy data set.

Traditionally the issue of the discipline of students within schools and institutions has created a tension between methods that restore order and value obedience over methods that teach new behaviors and encourage autonomy and an inner locus of control (Kohn, 1999). It remains a crucial issue to be analyzed in any deconstructive exercise or reconstruction of any new PBIS framework. In many ways using an ABA framework for understanding human behavior encourages the external control of behavior and de-emphasizes the development of autonomy and an inner locus of control. The method manipulates individuals to comply but does nothing to teach or practice new behaviors. Nor does it give reasons for the required behavior (Pink, 2009). These ways of constructing meaning around intervening upon children's behavior run counter to widely accepted framework of child psychological theory. Piaget and Erikson considered the concept of autonomy to be crucial in the development of the moral and intellectual development of children (Kamii, 1989). Yet the external implementation of an intervention is the antithesis of this idea. Likewise Piaget states specifically that: "Adults reinforce the child's natural heteronomy when they use rewards and punishment to reinforce desired behaviors thereby hindering the development of autonomy" (Kamii, 1989, pp. 47). Reward and punishment are often the mainstays of behavioral interventions' in schools (Kelsey, 2010). While external control is sometimes necessary in the classroom, it should not be the exclusive method of management (Knestrict, 2006). Behavioristic methods, "if you do this you get this", often will control behavior for short periods of time but they do nothing to change behavior (Deci, Koestner, & Ryan, 1999). This creates what Piaget called "heteronomy" or the external control of others and the preponderance of heteronomous control in schools contributed to the creation of students who were quite comfortable letting others control them intellectually and morally (Piaget 1965, 1973).

Psychology has returned to a more eclectic perspective that is reminiscent of its earlier years (Mills, 1998). However, in the field of PBIS behaviorism and its current day applied version, ABA, is alive and well. With this method comes the historical baggage that a more pure version of behaviorism brings with it. Mills (1998) stated that these prior commitments were still visible in all behavioristic frameworks. First is a view of the singularity of the method, a materialistic view that includes a deep suspicion and distrust of any other method of understanding human motivation and behavior especially if it involves the consideration of the inner workings of the human mind, internal motivations, or internal locus of control, and a reliance on a positivistic view of the world and the steadfast belief that truth can be quantified and known. It is a major theme of this text to make the argument that this narrow view of supporting individuals with behavioral challenges is limited and that a different and broader perspective is necessary to impact the development of students struggling with behavior.

Pillar Three—Oppression and the Explicit and Implicit Curriculum of Banking Education

Oppression is the term used to define the forces within a system that create and maintain injustice (Adams & Bell, 1997). It is hard to imagine a more unlikely place to find oppression and injustice then in a school with professionals struggling to make the lives of students better by intervening upon those struggling with chronic behavioral issues. The intentions of these professionals are good. The intentions of the theorists who developed PBIS were good as well. However, good intentions do not guarantee that that the outcomes are just and that harm is not occurring. Social Justice is defined as the fair and equitable distribution of resources with the imperative to address those who are least advantaged (Rawls, 2001). Also, social justice draws on the theories that affirm the importance of fair and equitable social processes (Young, 1990). Injustice occurs when differences in individuals are sorted and placed in a hierarchy that unequally confers power, social, and economic advantages based upon their place in the hierarchy (Bell, 2016). PBIS does just that. By placing students in the light of needing intervention, they are placed within the framework and in some instances placed on an accelerated path to special education identification.

Freire (1970) wrote of the idea of placing the oppressed at the center of their own learning and to develop a critical consciousness. Schooling in the United States and systems like PBIS support the status quo through both the implicit and explicit curriculum. Explicitly, those in power determine the behavioral norms of a school. The students rarely, if ever, participate in the development of those rules and norms. They are bribed and encouraged and earn privileges but are never allowed to forget who the "giver and the taker" is. Compliance and order are valued and the PBIS system attempts to ensure these norms. Implied in the use of PBIS are several unspoken and damaging messages. The first being, "we are in control of you." It may appear that you students have the ability to make choices within this system but in reality the cards are stacked and compliance trumps autonomy. There is also the message that there is no inherent value in being here and engaging in learning so we will pay you. In preparation for this book a teacher shared an analogy. Her observation was that PBIS and the behavior plans generated constitute nothing more than a glorified drug dealer and junkie relationship. The student becomes addicted to the external rewards and punishment and will not engage unless they are there. Rewards, like drugs, have a limited viability and the rewards, like the chemical being used, must increase over time. Her observation and indeed, the way she runs her school, show that there is another way. It looks very much like the "anti-banking" model described by Freire (1970) "the students-no longer docile listeners- are now critical co-investigators in dialog with teachers" (pp. 62).

Pillar Four—The Historical Significance of the Concept of Normalcy

Baker (2002) documented the historical influence of the eugenics movement of the 19th century and qualified two historically different types of eugenics. The first being the example set by Nazi Germany and the Holocaust. While this version never reached a hegemonic state in the truest sense of the word, it did create what Foucault (1979) called "dividing practices". This is the idea that people holding power will create technologies that will categorize, sort and create hierarchies. There has evolved a less virulent form, which Baker (2002) describes as the "New Eugenics". The general understanding of the concept of the "New" eugenics is:

> Constructing and privileging certain kinds of whiteness over certain kinds of color, certain kinds of masculinity over certain kinds of femininity, certain kinds of ability over "corporally anomalous" body and minds and tolerating only a narrow version of heteronormativity and religious practice. (p. 665)

Lowe (1997, 2000) identifies several areas of educational policy that serve to do this type of separating and privileging. His analysis gives evidence of the

continued survival and popularity of the "New" eugenics ideas as they relate
to normalcy are:

1) **Testing**—Ascertaining ability levels, IQ, behavioral deficits, documenting them and then using this data to label, place and medi-
calize. The PBIS process facilitates the process of collecting data as
educators move towards special education labeling and placement.
If the multitiered intervention model has failed to ameliorate the
behavioral issues identified then the special education process can
begin. It begins with more testing and assessment. The Educational
Team Report (ETR) once known as the multi-factored evaluation can
commence. The ETR can consist of reports by teachers; counselors
and school psychologists documenting the students present levels of
functioning. This would include multiple behavioral measures including the data collected during the failed intervention attempts during
PBIS. Once labeled individuals considered as "having" a disability
rarely achieve at the same level as before the labeling. In a positivist
environment what else can such techniques produce except to con-
firm historical stereotypes in those disposed to cling to them? Harry
and Klingner (2014) reported the following post schooling data:

   1. 73% of students labeled with LD were working post secondarily
   2. 50% of those with the EBD label were employed after schooling.
   3. 1/3 of all special education students did not graduate from high
   school
   4. 16 years later only 35% were employed with the LD label 25%
   with the ED label.

Giroux (1983) mentions the importance of developing research tools
that will uncover an understanding of the structural reproduction
of ideologies of difference and how they matter in the lives of both
the dominant and non-dominant group. Applied Behavioral Analysis would have us believe that school norms are the arbiters of what
"normal" is. However, if you look at who leads schools in the United
States and who leads most PBIS efforts, identification of special needs
and discipline efforts, they are predominantly white middle class men
and women creating a normative culture based upon their experience (Bornstein, 2017). Is it any wonder that under represented students make up the majority of discipline referrals, tier two and three

interventions and special education placements? Simply categorizing using "normalcy" as the measure allows those in power to determine what is "normal". Brown, Anderson, and De Pry (2015) identify PBIS as "best practice" for intervening on behaviors and it is a sanctioned method for identifying students with special needs. The authors state specifically that one of goals of the ABA based PBIS models was to "provide a life that was as *normalized* as possible through means that were culturally normalized as possible" (.United States Department of Education & Office of Civil Rights 2004).

2) **Differential Treatment**—differentiating individuals according to there cognitive ability, normative behavior or other socially constructed measure historically has resulted in those individuals being treated differently and placed somewhere else in the hierarchy. In the United States school systems one of the ways we differentiate is through PBIS and special education. Within the PBIS model the process begins by placing students within one of three tiers or levels. Each subsequent level lying within the model is providing more structure and more restrictiveness in an attempt to remediate the behavioral issue. Many believe that this is the first step in identifying students with special needs and indeed the data support this idea (Bornstein, 2017). Once on tier two and three the intervention plans can modify the day of the student dramatically. Students on these tiers can be bribed, or rewarded for behaviors that others must do without reinforcement (bribes) and the quality of their day can be much different from their fellow classmates. It is also a time where data is often collected to "prove" a disability exists. Once identified within the special education framework the curriculum becomes guided by the Individualized Education Plan (IEP) at this time the physical placement of the student may change. Behaviorally their treatment may change as well. There is evidence that poor, under represented students will be treated dramatically different then their white, upper class peers (Annamma, Morrison, & Jackson, 2014). This difference is also evident in the over representation of students of color and students who are poor in both PBIS and special education identification (Weber, 2009).

3) **The Quality of Home Life and Mothering**—has been identified as a way that schools separate out "problematic" children from others. Bornstein (2017) described a discussion that occurred in Intervention

Team Meetings clearly identifying chaotic home life and parenting concerns as viable data within a school based discussion of behavior. The cultural sensitivity and bias of such conversations is well documented (Coll & Pachter, 2002; Julian, McKenry, & McKelvey, 1994; Lareau & Horvat, 1999). When discussing discipline related interventions the population of the students being intervened upon in the United States are predominantly black, male and poor (Skiba, Michael, Nardo, & Peterson, 2002). The make up of the typical intervention assistance team is made up of teachers, school psychologists and administrators all of whom are predominantly white, middle class men and women (Rodriguez, 1983). The field of school psychology is made up of overwhelmingly white and middle class individuals (Curtis, Grier, Abshier, Sutton, & Hunley, 2002). The apparent lopsided representation of professionals in this process further illustrates the potential to create a hegemonic relationship between the core group interveners and the students they are assigned to help. In this hegemonic environment administrators and school psychologist spend most of their time simply trying to control behavior, separate, segregate normal children from abnormal children and not on trying to understand the diverse versions of family, parenting and home life that students manifest in school (Turner-Vorbeck, 2005).

Conclusion

The genealogy of PBIS is enmeshed with the history of behavior modification, learning theory and special education. The residue of these historical foundations cannot be escaped and are identifiable in the practice of PBIS today. The term "intervention" is defined as; "to involve oneself in a situation so as to alter or hinder an action or development" (American Heritage Dictionary, retrieved 5-7-2018). Historically PBIS is also inextricably tied to the applied version of behaviorism, Applied Behavioral Analysis. The legacy of this fundamental pillar of PBIS practice seems to emphasize the value of compliance and obedience at the expense of developing autonomy and an inner locus of control. Historically the schools are highly motivated to force students into compliance in order to maintain order and boost achievement scores. The use of PBIS, while well intentioned still produces unintended outcomes because of the implicit and explicit curriculum generated by its use. A more student centered socially just and relationship based system is called for.

There is what Baker (2002) calls a "new eugenics" by which children are not killed because of their differences from what the dominant culture sees as "normal" but they are marginalized, sorted, labeled and placed within the special education system allegedly to provide the academic and behavioral support they need (Baker, 2002). The realities are much different and the special education system, which PBIS is a part of, fails them and marginalizes them (Harry & Klingner, 2014). From a social justice perspective there are several issues that spring up by just looking critically at the historical development of the PBIS mode. The first of these is the valuing of obedience and compliance over autonomy. When a system facilitates a dependence upon external rewards we create what resembles a drug addiction for the student (Pink, 2009). A reinforcement schedule is set up but over time the student will need more of a reward to do the same task. There are people in our culture who require 24 hour a day external control for 365 days per year. They are called prisoners. Creating a dependence upon external control is not empowering students at all in fact it sets them up for failure when they realize, at some point in their life, that they will not be paid for completing tasks (Kohn, 1999). The development of autonomy and the ability to love to read or learn should be the reward. If rewards are necessary for students to learn or behave it begs the question of why? The next concern that is uncovered when looking at the historical development of the PBIS model is the valuing of control over real change and mastery of behaviors. The original purpose of the PBIS model was to teach new behaviors (Sugai & Simonsen, 2012). However, it is clear that if the student simply complies with the rules that will be more than enough to satisfy authorities. This begs the question 'if compliance is all we require are we creating autonomous thinkers and learners or just individuals who can follow rules? Some researchers have found that if we see schools as merely a way of indoctrinating workers for the economy, then compliance is more than enough (Giroux, 1983).

PBIS also encourages the marginalization of large groups of people and especially those in under-represented groups (Annamma et al., 2014; Bornstein, 2017). Many view the PBIS model historically as a way of facilitating special education labeling and placement. If we look at the statistical outcomes for those identified with special needs we see that many do not graduate or become contributing members of society after schooling (Harry & Klingner, 2014). Also, there is new data that shows the tremendous social isolation of those identified with special needs. Could providing real support that develops an internal locus of control and intellectual and emotional autonomy make students more able to cope (Kamii & Clark, 1993)?

Uncovering the history of PBIS has also shown that the framework, historically, is run by experts and the stakeholders are rarely meaningfully involved. This marginalization of parents and students in the direct processes that affect their personal development is one of the greatest social injustices uncovered by this deconstructive exercise. Legally, according to IDEA, parents have the ultimate ability to start or stop these processes at any point in time. Legally, according to IDEA students should also be involved where appropriate (U. S. Department of Education, 2012). That information about their power in these matters is not made known to them by the school district and often requires involvement of parent advocates and lawyers for them to become aware of their rights.

It was also shown that the PBIS model was developed in the shadow of special education and the medical model of disability and retains a significant bias towards special education and the identification of children (Dunlap et al., 2009). This is especially true of children with chronic behavioral issues. Whereas, students with significant behavioral issues were historically seen as "disturbing" and "disorderly". They are now, through the medicalization of the special education lens, are more often seen as "disturbed" and "disordered" indicating a shift from externally caused behavior to emotionally disturbed behavior (Bornstein, 2017). PBIS has encouraged the medicalization of severe behavior in schools (Skrtic, 1991). The frameworks of ABA, PBIS and special education itself are no longer challenged and are seen by teachers and parents alike, as a necessary process to go through to ameliorate chronic misbehavior. It is considered a "within the child" problem and the external causes of these behaviors, poverty, poor teaching, lack of engagement, boredom, pressure of standards based curriculum, are no longer considered factors when analyzing behavior in schools. Or are overlooked because of a fundamental attribution error (Fiedler & Semin, 1996). This is an issue that will be discussed in depth in Chapter five. PBIS and the behavioral strategies utilized as interventions, special education and the medical model it evolved from are taken as truth in education and are rarely questioned. As we uncover the layers of history leading to current day practice we see a need to question and examine these practices to determine whether individuals are being served by them or held down because of them.

References

Adams, M., Bell, L. and Griffin, P. 1997. *Teaching for diversity and social justice: A sourcebook*, New York: Routledge.

Alberto, P. A., & Troutman, A. C. (2012). Applied behavior analysis for teachers (9th ed.). Upper Saddle River, NJ: Prentice-Hall.

American Heritage Dictionary. (2018, May 11).

Anderson, J. L., Albin, R. W., Mesaros, R. A., Dunlap, G., & Morelli-Robbins, M. (1993). Issues in providing training to achieve comprehensive behavioral support. *Communicative Alternatives to Challenging Behavior: Integrating Functional Assessment and Intervention Strategies, 3*, 363–406.

Annamma, S., Morrison, D., & Jackson, D. (2014). Disproportionality fills in the gaps: Connections between achievement, discipline and special education in the School-to-Prison Pipeline. *Berkeley Review of Education, 5*(1).

Artiles, A. J., Harry, B., Reschly, D. J., & Chinn, P. C. (2002). Over-identification of students of color in special education: A critical overview. *Multicultural Perspectives, 4*(1), 3–10.

Axelrod, S. A. (1990). Myths that (mis)guide our profession. In A. C. Repp & N. N. Singh (Eds.), *Perspectives on the use of nonaversive and aversive interventions for persons with developmental disabilities* (pp. 59–72). Sycamore, IL: Sycamore.

Baker, B. (2002). The hunt for disability: The new eugenics and the normalization of school children. *Teachers College Record, 104*(4), 663–703.

Beyer, L., & Apple, M. (1988). Curriculum: Problems, politics and possibilities, Albany: State University of New York

Bornstein, J. (2017), Can PBIS Build Justice Rather Than Merely Restore Order?, in Nathern S. Okilwa, Muhammad Khalifa, Felecia M. Briscoe (ed.) *The School to Prison Pipeline: The Role of Culture and Discipline in School (Advances in Race and Ethnicity in Education, Volume 4)* Emerald Publishing Limited, pp. 135–167.

Brantlinger, E. (1997). Using ideology: Cases of non-recognition of the politics of research and practice in special education. *Review of Educational Research, 67*(4), 425–459.

Broderick, A., and Z. Leonoardo. 2016. "What a Good Boy: The Deployment and Distribution of "Goodness" as Ideological Property in Schools." In *DisCrit-Disability Studies and Critical Race Theory in Education,* edited by D. J.Connor, B. A. Ferri, and S. A. Annamma. New York: Teachers College Press.

Brown, F., Anderson, J., & De Pry, R. L. (Eds.). (2015). *Individual positive behavior supports: A standards-based guide to practices in school and community settings.* Baltimore: Paul H. Brookes Publishing Company.

Charney, R. S. (1998). Teaching children to care: Management in the responsive classroom. Greenfield, MA: Northeast Foundation for Children.

Christmas in Purgatory, YouTube, 2017.

Coll, C. G., & Pachter, L. M. (2002). Ethnic and minority parenting. In *Handbook of parenting: Social conditions and applied parenting* (pp. 1–20). Ed. Mark Bornstein, Lawrence Erlbaum and associates, Mahweh, NJ.

Colvin, G., Kame'enui, E. J., & Sugai, G. (1993). School-wide and classroom management: Reconceptualizing the integration and management of students with behavior problems in general education. *Education and Treatment of Children, 16*, 361–381.

Colvin, G., Sugai, G., & Kame'enui, E. J. (1994). *Proactive schoolwide discipline: Implementation manual*. Project PREPARE. Behavioral Teaching and Research, College of Education, University of Oregon, Eugene.

Curtis, M. J., Grier, C., Abshier, D. W., Sutton, N. T., & Hunley, S. (2002). NASP demographic study: School psychology: Turning the corner into the twenty-first century. Communiqué, 30, 8.

Davis, L. J. (Ed.). (2016). *The disability studies reader.*Routledge, New York, NY.

Deci, E. L., Koestner, R., & Ryan, R. M. (1999). A meta-analytic review of experiments examining the effects of extrinsic rewards on intrinsic motivation. Psychological Bulletin 125. no. 659.

Donnellan, A. M., Mirenda, P. L., Mesaros, R. A., & Fassbender, L. L. (1984). Analyzing the communicative functions of aberrant behavior. *Journal of the Association for Persons with Severe Handicaps*, 9(3), 201–212.

Evans, S. W. (1999). Mental health services in schools: Utilization, effectiveness, and consent. *Clinical Psychology Review*, 19, 165–178.

Fairbanks, S., Sugai, G., Guardino, D., & Lathrop, M. (2007). Response to intervention: Examining classroom behavior support in second grade. *Exceptional Children*, 73(3), 288–310.

Fiedler, K., & Semin, G. R. (1996). *Applied social psychology*. London: SAGE Publications Ltd.

Foucault, M. (1977). *Discipline and punish: The birth of the prison*. New York, NY: Pantheon Books.

Freire, P. (1970). *Pedagogy of the oppressed*. New York, NY: Continuum.

Gaylord-Ross, R. (1980). A decision model for the treatment of aberrant behavior in applied settings. In W. Sailor, B. Wilcox, & L. Brown (Eds.), *Methods of instruction for severely handicapped students* (pp. 135–158). Baltimore, MD: Brookes.

Giroux, H. (1983). Theories of reproduction and resistance in the new sociology of education: A critical analysis. *Harvard Educational Review*, 53(3), 257–293.

Gresham, F. M. (1991). Conceptualizing behavior disorders in terms of resistance to intervention. School Psychology Review, 20, 23–36.

Harry, B., & Klingner, J. (2014). *Why are so many minority students in special education?* Teachers College Press.

Horner, R. H., Dunlap, G., Koegel, R. L., Carr, E. G., Sailor, W., Anderson, J., … O'Neill, R. E. (1990). In support of integration for people with severe problem behaviors: A response to four commentaries. *Journal of the Association for Persons with Severe Handicaps*, 15(3), 145–147.

Iwata, B. A., Dorsey, M. F., Slifer, K. J., Bauman, K. E., & Richman, G. S. (1982). Toward a functional analysis of self-injury. *Analysis and Intervention in Developmental Disabilities*, 2(1), 3–20.

Julian, T. W., McKenry, P. C., & McKelvey, M. W. (1994). Cultural variations in parenting: Perceptions of Caucasian, African-American, Hispanic, and Asian-American parents. *Family Relations*, 30–37.

Kamii, C. (1989). *Young children continue to reinvent arithmetic*. New York, NY: Teachers College Press.

Kamii, C., & Clark, F. B. (1993). Autonomy: The importance of a scientific theory in education reform. *Learning and Individual Differences, 5*(4), 327–340.

Kelsey, J. (2010). The negative impact of rewards and ineffective praise on student motivation. *ESSAI, 8,* Article 24.

Kincaid, D., Dunlap, G., Kern, L., Lane, K. L., Bambara, L. M., Brown, F., . . . Knoster, T. P. (2016). Positive behavior support: A proposal for updating and refining the definition. Journal of Positive Behavior Interventions, 18, 69–73.

Knestrict, T. (2006). Rules, rituals and routines program guide and study guide. Learning Seed Publications. Learning Seed Publishing, Lake Zurich, Ill.

Knestrict, T. (2016). The special education industrial complex. *Journal of Behavioral and Social Sciences, 3*(4), 201–211.

Kohn, A. (1999). *Punished by rewards: The trouble with gold stars, incentive plans, A's, praise, and other bribes.* New York, NY: Houghton Mifflin Harcourt.

Lareau, A., & Horvat, E. M. (1999). Moments of social inclusion and exclusion race, class, and cultural capital in family-school relationships. *Sociology of Education, 72,* 37–53.

Lowe, R. (1997). *Schooling and social change, 1964–1990.* London: Routledge.

Lowe, R. (2000). Eugenics, scientific racism and education: Has anything changed in one hundred years? In M. Crotty, J. Germov, & G. Rodwell (Eds.), *A race for a place: Eugenics, Darwinism, and social thought and practice in Australia* (pp. 207–220). Newcastle, NSW: The University of Newcastle.

Merrell, K. W., & Buchanan, R. (2006). Intervention selection in school-based practice: Using public health models to enhance systems capacity of schools. *School Psychology Review, 35,* 167–180.

Meyer, L. H., & Evans, I. M. (1989). *Nonaversive intervention for behavior problems: A manual for home and community.* Baltimore: Brookes.

Mills, J. A. (1998). *Control: A history of behavioral psychology.* New York: NYU Press.

Morrow, R. A., & Brown, D. D. (1994). *Critical theory and methodology* (Vol. 3). Thousand Oaks California: Sage. Oxford English Dictionary of Critical theory.

Pas, E. T., Bradshaw, C. P., & Mitchell, M. M. (2011). Examining the validity of office discipline referrals as an indicator of student behavior problems. *Psychology in the Schools, 48*(6), 541–555.

Piaget, J. (1965). *The moral judgment of the child.* New York, NY: Free Press. (Originally published 1938).

Piaget, J. (1973). *To understand is to invent.* New York, NY: Grossman. (Originally published 1948).

Pink, D. H. (2009). *Drive: The surprising truth about what motivates us.* New York: Penguin.

Pugach, M., & Johnson, L. (1995). *Collaboration as specific problem solving, in collaborative practitioners, collaborative schools.* Denver, CO: Love Publishing Company.

Rawls, J. (2001). *Justice and fairness: A restatement.* Cambridge, MA: Harvard University Press.

Renzaglia, A., & Bates, P. (1983). Socially appropriate behavior. In M. E. Snell (Ed.), *Systematic instruction of the moderately and severely handicapped* (2nd ed., pp. 314–356). Columbus, OH: Merrill

Rodriguez, F. (1983). *Educational in a multicultural society.* Washington, DC: University Press of America.

Skiba, R. J., Michael, M., Nardo, A. C., & Peterson, R. L. (2002). The color of discipline: Sources of racial and gender disproportionality in school punishment. *The Urban Review, 34*(4), 317–342.

Skinner, B. F. (2014). Retrieved from http://www.biography.com/people/bf-skinner-9485671

Skrtic, T. (1991). The special education paradox: Equity as the way to excellence. *Harvard Educational Review, 61*(2), 148–120.

Sugai, G., & Horner, R. H. (1999). Discipline and behavioral support: Practices, pitfalls, & promises. *Effective School Practices, 17*(4), 10–22.

Sugai, G., & Simonsen, B. (2012). *Positive behavioral interventions and supports: History, defining features, and misconceptions.* Center for PBIS & Center for Positive Behavioral Interventions and Supports, University of Connecticut.

Thomas, G., & Loxley, T. (2001). *Deconstructing special education and constructing inclusion.* Buckingham: Open University Press.

Thorndike, E. L. (1911). *Animal intelligence: Experimental studies.* Macmillan.

Turner-Vorbeck, T. A. (2005). Expanding multicultural education to include family diversity. *Multicultural Education, 13*(2), 6–10.

United States Department of Education & Office of Civil Rights. (2004). Reauthorization of PL108–446.

United States Department of Education & Office of Civil Rights. (2012). *Helping to ensure equal access to education.* Washington, DC: Author.

Walker, H. M., Horner, R. H., Sugai, G., Bullis, M., Sprague, J. R., Bricker, D., & Kaufman, M. J. (1996). Integrated approaches to preventing antisocial behavior patterns among school-age children and youth. *Journal of Emotional and Behavioral Disorders, 4,* 193–256.

Watson, J. B. (1958). *Behaviorism.* New York: Transaction Publishers.

Weber, M. C. (2009). The IDEA eligibility mess. *Buffalo Law Review, 57,* 83.

Young, I. M. (1990). *Justice and the politics of difference.* Princeton, NJ: Princeton University Press.

Zins, J. E., Curtis, M., Graden, J., & Ponti, C. (1989). *Using consultation to provide services to all students, in helping students succeed in the regular classroom.* San Francisco, CA: Jossey-Bass Publishers.

· 2 ·

DECONSTRUCTION OF THE
BEHAVIORAL FOUNDATION OF PBIS

Social Justice Points of Chapter Two:

1. *Applied Behavioral Analysis emphasizes difference and is premised upon unequal relationships of power.*
2. *Special Education further supports these unequal relationships.*
3. *Applied Behavioral Analysis values obedience over autonomy.*
4. *Applied Behavioral Analysis constructs normalcy using a white, middle-class framework that emphasizes compliance.*

The scope of this book does not allow us to go into the depth of the research that advocates the abandonment of behavioristic strategies to motivate individuals. Pink (2009) and Kohn (1999) dove deeply into the research of Deci, Koestner, and Ryan (2001) and the application of these tenets with Deming models (1986). However, there are six themes that are consistent throughout this research that speak to the negative effects of the applied use of behaviorism within the PBIS model. These tenets also illustrate the social justice inequities that are manifest in these techniques. The first is the "Hedonic Adaptation" (Brickman & Campbell, 1981). Hedonic adaptation speaks to the idea that a pleasurable stimulus (reward) has decreasing pleasurable effect over time. If a behavioral intervention plan is based upon rewards or punishments the effects of these will fade over time, requiring an increase of pay-off or negative reinforcement to have the same effect on the individual (Frederick & Loewenstein, 1999). This results in ever-growing rewards and ever-harsher negative reinforcement or punishment. The second theme that manifests in PBIS and schools in general is that behavioral strategies create unequal relationships between the intervener and the intervened upon. Kohn (1999) stated that in this type of relationship the teacher and student are of unequal status, one subjugated by the other. The term "intervention" itself denotes something being done "to" the child. The professional adult has greater power than the child. This type of dynamic encourages the use of external control and creates what Pink (2009) characterizes as an archaic system that suits 19th- and 20th-century industrial models better than 21st-century schools and business by encouraging compliance rather than responsibility.

The third theme is the tendency of external rewards and punishment inherent in an ABA framework, which tends to lessen the quality of the task being externally controlled. Deci et al. (2001) found that when externally manipulated, subjects tended to perform just well enough to earn the reward and no better. Boggiano and Barrett (1992) found that when fourth grade students were externally controlled to complete a set of problem-solving tasks they used less sophisticated learning strategies and scored lower on standardized test than did children who were learning for its own sake. Amabile (1993) also found that creativity is significantly reduced when external controls are implemented. There is an ever-increasing amount of data in and out of the school context that show that this type of externally controlled framework is less effective at motivating individuals, discourages creativity, has a downward achievement curve, and creates reward-addicted people (Kohn, 1999).

The fourth theme is that it discourages what Piaget (1965, 1973), Kami (1989), and Erikson (1953) defined as autonomy. They wrote about the different types of autonomy, which included intellectual and moral autonomy. Piaget (1973; Kami, 1989) stated specifically that it was education's purpose to create morally and intellectually autonomous students.

Fifth, there is awkwardness to implementing these external systems of surveillance necessitated by externally driven models of controlling behavior. A glance at an ABA textbook will instantly show the level of tediousness required to design and implement a behavior management plan as dictated by ABA methods. It is clear that the designers and writers of these books were primarily researchers and not actual teachers in a classroom (Alberto & Troutman, 2006). Managing 30 students, teaching six different subjects, and managing a behavior management plan based in ABA techniques are impossible, impractical, and almost never happen. What you do get is a rudimentary form of behaviorism, based in rewards and punishment, that is designed for eliciting obedience and compliance in an effort to improve academic achievement as measured by mandated standardized testing. It also dictates assessment of the effectiveness of these plans by single measures like Office Discipline Referrals (ODR), a practice that illustrates the motivations of the school professionals in designing behavior-based systems, which are obedience, compliance, and silence so as to improve test scores. These types of measures also encourage the movement of individuals with particularly problematic behaviors through the three-tiered system and onto the special education process to again ensure obedience, compliance, silence, and ultimately removal if interventions are deemed ineffective.

The sixth and final idea is the concept of Fundamental Attribution Error (FAE) when using the PBIS model that is guided by ABA. FAE is defined by Harman (1999) as the error of ignoring situational factors and overconfidently assuming that the distinctive behaviors are due to an agent's distinctive character traits. This error motivates behavior planning that looks at internal states rather than considering external or contextual variables or even teacher behavior or bias. The problem is within the child so the plan will encourage changing the child. There is also evidence that this model also encourages what Skiba et al (2006) and Bornstein (2017) characterize as pathologizing behavior and the disabling of students with behavioral difficulties.

The purpose of this chapter is to deconstruct the applied version of behaviorism, commonly called Applied Behavioral Analysis (ABA), as used within the PBIS model. Pink (2009) states:

> We can cling to a view of human motivation that is grounded more in old habits than in modern science. Or we can listen to the research, drag our personal and professional practices into the 21st century, and craft a new operating system to help ourselves, our companies, our schools and our world to work a little better. (p. 79)

It is also the purpose of this chapter to illustrate why the continued use of ABA within the PBIS model creates hegemonic and discriminatory systems and creates a segregated and unequal hierarchy that can negatively affect the development and life outcomes for children.

Hedonic Adaptation—Increasing Rewards/ Ever-Harsher Punishment

Hedonic Adaptation refers to an action or process or mechanism that reduces the effects of constant or repeated stimulus (Frederick & Loewenstein, 1999). For example, if a behavior plan provides primary reinforcers for "on task" behavior and a negative consequence (loss of bonus points) for not remaining on task, Hedonic Adaptation would say that the effect of both the positive and negative reinforcement would diminish over time due to the brain's adaptation process. This is similar to the effects that cocaine has on the body. Over time the body requires more of the drug to obtain the same "high." Bribes in the classroom are like this as well. The more a child can earn for completing a task the more reward they will require, over time.

This type of adaptation has further costs as well. Brickman and Campbell (1981) talk about the "hedonic treadmill" that describes when rewards and goals that have been met give way to indifference or even dissatisfaction. The concept was modified by Eysenck & Eysenck, (1975) British psychologists, to become the current "hedonic adaptation theory," which compares the pursuit of happiness to a person on a hedonic treadmill who has to keep walking just to stay in the same place. Sometimes the attainment of a goal or the earning of a behavioral contract can seem like almost a letdown (Sciovsky, 1971). It is thought that this has to do with the fact that students tend to enjoy the process and the attention that behavioral plans provide and those benefits stop at the attainment of the contract, which is further evidence pointing toward the importance of relationships in the behavioral support process.

The adaptation works toward the negative as well. If students fail to earn their contract or fail to change the behaviors being rewarded there is usually a consequence delivered by the manipulator of the behavioral plan. Negative reinforcements also lose impact over time, often eliciting an inflation of the harshness (Koob, Stinus, Le Moal, & Bloom, 1989). In the school context there is seldom a systematic or thoughtful change in these contingencies. Frustration and anger of the teacher often motivate an increase in harshness.

The combination of the decrease of effectiveness of external rewards for behavior combined with the addictive qualities of contingent-based behavior plans makes for behavioral plans that look more and more like an interaction between a drug dealer and an addict. Like in a dealer/addict relationship the "dealer" is in control and the addict is not. The addict is dependent upon the dealer to provide product in order for the addict's day to proceed. The dealer can manipulate the addict to behave the way they want them to. However, over time, the addict requires more and more of the drug to get high, eventually building a tolerance that requires the addict to be rewarded with the drug more and more just to survive. The addict is no longer using the drug to get high; they now use just to survive. Teachers often bribe students to complete work, get better grades, and behave in a certain way. Students are rewarded when they comply. At first the student is motivated by the reward. Over time, however, the reward is no longer effective and a new more stimulating reward is necessary. The rewards inflate and the effect diminishes (Brickman & Campbell, 1981), leaving a student with the need to be "paid" or rewarded for doing the simplest task and earning a reward that has grown out of proportion. The reverse is also true. The negative consequences become harsher and more punitive in nature and usually end in the removal of the student from the classroom (Bornstein, 2017).

Unequal Relationships
(Rewards Damage Relationships)

It is worth restating the definition of ABA as quoted by Alberto and Troutman (2006).

> The systematic application of behavioral principles to change socially significant behaviors to a meaningful degree. Research tools enable users of these principles to verify a functional relation between a behavior and an intervention. (p. 403)

I would begin deconstructing this definition and noting the cultural bias it contains. Who decides what "socially significant" actually is? "To a meaningful degree" is vague and ironically is not observable or measureable. The model is inherently dependent upon an authority making these judgments, and it is well documented that the predominant social class, culture, and gender of most teachers are counter to the experiences of many of our children in public schools (Ursavaş & dan Reisoglu, 2017).

A school visited in preparation for this book developed three-tiered PBIS model that they had implemented at the beginning of the previous school year. As part of the tier one system they rewarded students randomly for appropriate behaviors teachers saw. Very often these were given for appropriate hallway behavior or kindness witnessed by a teacher. Students were given "I Caught You" (ICY) tickets, which could be turned in for bonus points at the end of each day and spent at the school store. Upon leaving the school one day there was a small girl crying in the hallway. When asked what was wrong she said that she didn't earn any ICY tickets and she didn't think her teacher liked her. Another student was flaunting her ICY tickets and singing, "I'm good. I'm good. You're not! You're not."

This real-life example illustrates two different ways these systems can begin to degrade and diminish relationships. Not just the student/teacher relationship but also the student-to-student relationships. Complaints of unequal treatment and playing favorites are common (Zedlow, 1976). As a rule the competition that this type of system engenders is not conducive for optimal learning or the development of a kind and caring community (Kohn, 1999). The central message implicitly sent by the utilization of these types of systems is that all of your classmates should be seen as potential obstacles to one's own success. Students may start viewing their classmates and their teacher with suspicion, contempt, or envy (Kohn, 1992). According to a series of studies by Ames (1978) people attribute the results of a competition like this to attributes beyond their control. Hence, many kids choose to not compete (Zubin, 1932).

In a study on school culture Libbey (2004) found that if the students felt that they were being treated fairly by staff and teachers, as it relates to school discipline, they were more engaged as learners and their achievement levels rose. It was also found that if there was not a "contingent feeling" to the school climate, teachers were genuine in their treatment of students. This positively impacted school climate, student engagement, and school participation. Lee (2012) in a study with 147 schools and over 3000 students found that a more responsive classroom technique and a more authoritative teacher–student relationship are correlated with higher achievement, greater school engagement, and a stronger bond between school and student. It is well established that contingency-based reward systems, which place a teacher in the role of "giver" or "taker" diminish trust between the teacher and student and create an environment where the student seeks only to "win" the reward (Kohn, 1999).

An atmosphere of nurturing or "emotional responsiveness" is needed to an academic and emotionally enabling environment (Elliot, McKevitt, & DiPerna, 2002). Contingency-driven models that coerce behavior do more damage to the student/teacher relationship than the system does good. Contingencies and responsiveness are mutually exclusive in terms of developing an optimal environment for trusting relationships and optimal academic engagement. Rosario Counseling (2016) defines responsiveness as cultivating the ability to give a meaningful reaction to the feelings of another person in the moment of their experience. It is about making a meaningful connection, validating the fact that they feel a certain way, and communicating your acknowledgement. Core values of effective schools and classrooms reflect this fundamental point. They develop trust and a high level of cooperation. When there is a high level of trust and a high level of cooperation in any system, synergy is the product. To put it simply, synergy means two or more trusting individuals working together are better than one person working alone. Synergy is the habit of creative cooperation. It is teamwork, open-mindedness, and finding new and individually derived solutions to problems. This process is significantly different than the current PBIS model that emphasizes the experts' view and judgment about the child, independent of the child (Covey, 1987). The Responsive Classroom (Charney, 1998) is a program developed by the Northeast Foundation that holds these truths at the core of their practices. Strategies like the morning meeting, collaborative rule development, and self-guided time outs work toward teaching behaviors that mold to the group's ideas of "appropriate." There is student buy-in because they are the authors and the participants in the system. It is not externally controlled; it is monitored and developed by the community that includes the teacher and the students.

Foucault (1977) was particularly concerned with the creation of unequal power relationships that are created and encouraged by what he termed "the human sciences." This is defined as bodies of knowledge or discourses that have man as their subject and create a regime of power that controls and describes human behavior in terms of norms by defining what is normal (Foucault, 1977). The power to define these parameters and control where a student goes to school and under what circumstances is a justice issue and begs further analysis. Especially when the entire framework within which these decisions are being made is validated by the hegemonic belief in science to determine truth. Bornstein (2017) is concerned with the "school to prison" pipeline and considers PBIS as a tool in what Foucault defined as the development of the "carceral system." Foucault was talking about the development of the prison system but his analysis can serve as a template for the development of the PBIS/Special Education Hierarchy. These can be seen as systems of discipline, acting upon individuals, meant to define normal, and place individuals at varying distances from normal (Foucault, 1977). This interactive pattern, with adults placing children within the PBIS framework, and the special education hierarchy looming in the distance, creates an unequal and socially unjust relationship between teachers and students, a relationship characterized by control, discipline, and the threat of further restrictive placement and a label that has been shown to be counterproductive once it is assigned (Fletcher, Coulter, Reschly, & Vaughn, 2004).

Kills Quality and Creativity

In preparation for this book several Intervention Assistance Team (IAT) meetings were observed. An urban school in Cincinnati is of particular interest. This particular school followed a very well-defined, three-tiered intervention model and also had formed an active IAT. They were problem solving and developing tier two and three interventions. A tier three plan in particular was addressing the behavior of a third grade student who was displaying a consistent pattern of "off task behavior" at which time his behavior would escalate to the point of the student being removed from the classroom and sent to the office. The team developed a plan that targeted the "on task" behavior and sought to increase the "time on task" from a one-minute chunk of time, which is how long he was observed to able to engage, to five minutes. Also, they sought to decrease the "acting out" behavior that was documented when he began to get frustrated and his behavior escalated. For every minute beyond the initial minute of on task behavior that the teacher witnessed the student earned a "bonus buck" (money used to buy treat at the end of the day). For every minute beyond that initial minute he also earned another "bonus buck" for using an indoor voice, sitting quietly, and not physically acting out in anger or frustration. After three weeks of being on the plan the intervention team documented fewer incidents of acting out behavior and an increased time on task to five minutes and classified the intervention as a success.

However, when we looked at the quality of the work completed during this time it was far below the level of work he was capable of or was even completing before the intervention was started. Also, while there was a decrease in acting out behavior as defined by the intervention plan there was an increase of more passive aggressive behaviors. In addition, his behavior in other classes with other teachers was markedly worse. This pattern of a decrease in quality of work is a pattern that is well documented in the literature (Kohn, 1999; Pink, 2009).

A Functional Behavioral Assessment (FBA) is supposed to be utilized to determine the function or purpose of the behavior. FBA is defined as *a* procedure designed to ascertain the purpose or reason for behaviors displayed by individuals with severe behavioral issues.

But even this strategy looks primarily at the student and the student's choices of behavior given a specific context. It is incumbent on the child to learn new behaviors rather than the context changing. This, I believe, is a major flaw of PBIS currently. Teachers, administrators, and school psychologists often have tunnel vision and see only the child's behavior and not the possible teacher or ecological variables that may be causing these choices.

Beginning in the 1960s researchers were discovering the counterproductive outcomes of using punishment and rewards of any kind on the quality of the work produced when there were external rewards promised. Miller and Estes (1961) conducted a study that asked 72 nine-year-old boys to look at pictures of two faces that differed slightly. Thinking that offering a reward would make the boys more likely to pick out the differences, she offered one group small monetary rewards for their work. The other group she offered nothing but feedback on whether they were correct or not. The group offered only feedback were much more adept at the task and scored higher in the exercise.

In 1962 Glucksberg (1962) conducted an experiment with 128 college-age men and women. They were all provided a set of materials that included a box, candle matches, thumbtacks and were told to mount the candle to the wall. One group was told they could earn $5, $10, $20 if they succeeded. The results were the same. Those working for money took 50% longer to solve the puzzle and demonstrated less creative problem solving while working.

Spence (1970) found that when participants were offered a reward for correctly identifying a correct word in a word puzzle the group offered rewards got fewer of the answers correct, prompting Spence (1971) to say "Rewards have effects on performance that we are only beginning to understand." Viesti (1971) in another study found that offering rewards decreased the accuracy of solutions of puzzles solved by participants. He doubled the reward and got the exact same results. Deci (1971) and Lepper, Greene, and Nisbett (1973) all had similar results with similar tasks, prompting Lepper to qualify his findings as "puzzling." Kohn (1999) concluded that by the 1980s anyone who kept up with this type of research would have found it impossible to claim that the best way to get people to perform well was to dangle a reward in front of them.

In the 1990s and beyond researchers in other areas of study have landed upon these same findings. The economists Ariely, Gneezy, Lowenstein, and Mazar (2005) found that pay for performance incentive plans have a long-term negative effect on the quality of the work performed. They stated, "Our results challenge (the idea of rewards improving performance). One cannot assume that raising incentives always improves performance. In many instances—contingent incentives—the cornerstone of how businesses attempt to motivate employees—may be a losing proposition" (p. 7).

Studies conducted over the same period of time also found that external rewards and punishments decreased creativity dramatically and seemed to have a distracting effect on the creative thought process in people. Amabile, Hennessey, and Grossman (1986; Amabile, 1993) discovered that when professional artists do work on commission it is generally seen as less creative; whether it is a writer or a visual artist, the results were the same.

Condry (1977) succinctly concluded that people who are offered rewards tend to:

> Choose easier tasks, are less efficient in using the information that is available to solve problems, and tend to be answer oriented and more illogical in their problem solving strategies. They seem to work harder and produce more activity, but the activity is of lower quality, contains more errors, and is more stereotyped and less creative than the work of comparable non-rewarded subjects working on the same problems. (pp. 471–472)

Discourages Autonomy

Perhaps the most powerful argument against the use of behaviorally based interventions becomes obvious when we look at how these methods affect a child's autonomy and sense of self-control. There is no more important issue than autonomy in terms of a social justice perspective. The control of others by someone above us in the social hierarchy is by definition a social justice issue and the use of behavioral strategies and a behavioristic worldview perpetuates this type of control and the student's comfort with this control. Autonomy is "governing oneself." The opposite of autonomy is "heteronomy," which is defined as making decisions dependent on external rewards or threats of punishment (Piaget, 1965). Piaget defined two types of autonomy. There is moral autonomy and intellectual autonomy. Moral autonomy is defined as an individual making choices based on what they believe to be the right and moral thing to do, independent of rewards or threats of punishments (Kami, 1989). Kami (1989) uses several examples of individuals who were morally autonomous and made decisions in their life in spite of great threats to their safety. Martin Luther King Jr. is an example she draws upon. King continued to pursue socially just goals even though his life and the lives of his family were threatened.

This is an important concept because many times children's behavior in schools is completely dependent upon the system of rewards and punishments that exist within the three tiers of intervention. In a behaviorist perspective the reason a certain behavior is demanded is rarely talked about or discussed with the student. There is usually only the expected behavior and the positive or negative reinforcement that follows the student's choice. One of the biggest complaints of a behavioristic framework is the lack of language involved in implementation. Vygotsky (1978) makes this point several times in his work, stating that new learning (behavior change) is always accompanied by new language acquisition. Also, how is the student supposed to construct an understanding of what is right and what is wrong unless there is discussion about these issues? According to both Piaget (1965) and Vygotsky (1978), all new learning is a result of discussion that assists children in making sense of the world.

The second type of autonomy that Piaget wrote about is intellectual autonomy. This is defined as thinking independently and confidently independent of rewards, punishment, or pressure from others (Kami, 1989). This type of autonomy can be seen in students who understand concepts so deeply and so well that they not only "know" the correct answer but also can defend it and explain how they came to that understanding. Piaget believed that both moral and intellectual autonomy were the ultimate goals of education (Piaget, 1932/65).

When we ask what facilitates the development of heteronomy in children Piaget explained that it was the use of rewards and punishment and external rewards in general that fostered the child's natural heteronomy and discouraged both moral and intellectual autonomy. The learning of anything new, and this includes learning new ways of behaving, is linked to understanding the expectations and understanding the reasons for those expectations. This doesn't happen by providing only rules and consequences. The child through an exchange of perspectives and viewpoints constructs the understanding. When the child sees the reason and is autonomously convinced of its credibility then they will do what is asked independent of rewards or punishments (Kami, 1989). These types of methods encourage not only autonomy but also responsibility and, at the same time, discourage the necessity for obedience-driven methods like rewards and threats of punishment.

Human beings have an internal need to be autonomous, self–determined, and connected to each other. When this drive is liberated, people achieve more and live richer lives (Pink, 2009). Deci and Ryan (2008) ceased using the terms internal or external locus of control. They now only use "Controlled" or "Autonomous." They found that when companies used an autonomous model of employee motivation, they had four times the rate of growth and one-third the turnover. Deci and Ryan (2008) also emphasize the power of an autonomous-driven model to help individuals develop relationships with one another. They state that this is more likely to happen in autonomous-driven systems because the individuals do not see each other as obstacles to their own success anymore. In fact, they begin to see the value in collaboration and the importance of nurturing and supportive relationships (Baglieri, 2008).

In the classroom, management models that begin not with the ubiquitous building wide reward system but with morning meetings, daily check ins, and an emphasis on personal contact—not adherence to rules—encourage positive relationships, caring, and support. Kohn (1995) finds that these types of methods and ways of thinking help develop kids who care about each other and are more prosocial in orientation. He also states that the classroom environments are more civil and less reliant on external control. These findings are supported by the work of Gartrell (2002) as well as the work of the Northeast Foundation and the Responsive Classroom (Charney, 1998).

If the rewards are offered in limited quantity and the students see each other as obstacles to winning the reward, they will compete with each other. Competition can devalue community (Kohn, 1990). If the point of the autonomous-driven system is to provide a supportive and caring system of individuals that help each other learn and grow, then the rewards and punishments are not necessary and in fact are counterproductive.

This is summed up by Pink (2009):

> One reason high achievers and (competitive students) are often depressed is because they are not developing good relationships. They are busy making (progress towards their own goals) achieving, making less room for love, attention, caring and empathy. The things that make life meaningful. (p. 60)

They are also the things that make an internal locus of control possible (Scheerer, Maddux, & Mercandante, 1982).

If we are committed to looking at the issue of PBIS using a social justice lens, then the use of these behavioral strategies should raise lots of red flags. The use of ABA is ubiquitous and it is not questioned. The use of all obedience-driven models is also not questioned because it is perceived to give us the results we want, which is silence for more teaching and higher test scores. A red flag should also be raised because of the unequal relationships that these methods incur. When we have a teacher cohort that consists predominantly of white middle-class women teaching predominantly poor underrepresented groups of students, these relationships take on a new meaning and we should be concerned. Finally, if the obedience-driven models encourage the development of heteronomous individuals who do not question authority and who lack intellectual autonomy and rigor they are ripe for exploitation and more control.

Awkwardness of Using the System

Riffel (2007) provides a template for the way behavior plans and FBAs should proceed. The process begins with a behavioral assessment, or data collection procedure that identifies target behaviors and then asks the teacher to identify possible reasons the student is choosing this behavior to get a specific need met. Once the reason is hypothesized then the antecedent for the behavior is named and the functional reinforcement the child receives as a result of that behavior choice. This is inherently a behavioristic framework for identifying and understanding behaviors. This framework, while it pays lip service to identifying contextual variables, still only identifies single target behaviors at a time. The resulting behavior plans will reflect this and typically will develop around the behavior and offer a reward for the decrease in said behavior or a consequence for continuing to use this behavior. In practice there is rarely a significant discussion about any contextual or external child variables. The reason for this is obvious to anyone who has taught. There is no time for this type of analysis. The quickest and surest way to control this behavior is with the threat of the stick or the allure of a carrot. Teachers just want the behavior to stop so they can teach. Or, they want the child to be removed from the class so they can teach. Or, they have received complaints from other parents in the room about the inappropriate behaviors from the student on the behavior plan and they are even more motivated to control this behavior so it stops. If your job depends upon rising test scores, then you are highly motivated for disruptive behaviors to stop or the disruptive child to be removed from class. As a principal, whose job depends upon rising test scores, you are also highly motivated to stop these disruptive behaviors or remove the disruptive student from the class. It is interesting to note that when a student has a reading difficulty or a math deficit, teachers will go to great lengths to remediate, support, and otherwise assist the student to catch up. However, when it comes to behavioral issues teachers rarely do anything but reward, punish, or remove these students. It has been well established in the literature that the possible negative outcomes of this process are overwhelmingly students from under-represented groups and particularly African-American boys. This is impactful on several levels, the least of which is the established connection between the PBIS process and the "school to prison pipeline" (Bornstein, 2017).

Within the PBIS framework there is a standing committee called the IAT. It is recommended that the IAT have an administrator, school psychologist, counselor, classroom teacher, intervention specialist, and whomever else the team views as beneficial to the problem-solving and planning process. The student is said to be able to participate if the team feels it is appropriate (Pugach & Johnson, 1995). Students and parents are rarely involved. The framework of the IAT is set up using a behaviorist perspective, and the primary purpose of the group is to establish the function of the targeted behaviors being documented and to develop a behavior plan that addresses these specific behaviors and provides a menu of reinforcement and consequences to diminish the frequency of the identified behaviors and replacement of these behaviors with more socially appropriate and less disruptive ones. One of the primary targets of the IAT and indeed of PBIS in general is to prevent special education identification. It is a very tedious process and rarely addresses all of the targeted behaviors and rarely addresses replacement behaviors in any meaningful way.

There are 10 questions that need to be asked to determine if the IAT is functioning in a socially just way and has the best interest of the children in mind. I also believe that these questions will allow a school to honestly reflect on differentiated treatment of underrepresented students, which has clearly been identified in the literature (Bornstein, 2017; Harry & Klingner, 2014; Kavale, 1990; Klingner & Bianco, 2006; Krezmien et al., 2006).

1) Does the culture of the school and the PBIS/IAT team use the process to prevent special education identification and placement?
2) Historically what is the percentage of identification/placement of children brought to the team?
3) Who is on this team?
4) Does the team include a diverse group of individuals?
5) Is there a clearly defined process and timeline for referral and interventions that is followed?
6) Is the team consciously addressing contextual variables including teacher behavior, school culture, and learning issues?
7) Is there a well-defined special education culture in the school? In other words, does the team see a difference in kids who are identified or "disabled" and "typically" developing kids?

8) Are the members of the IAT aware of the negative outcomes of identifying students with a disability?
9) Is there a high level of pressure on teachers because of the testing culture?
10) Do educators in the building believe that the best place for a child to be is with their typically developing peers?

At the classroom level administering a tedious behavior plan for one student is difficult enough. However, when you have three to five students on plans and you must teach 25 other students, with the pressures of the testing culture it becomes difficult at best and impossible at worst. Below there is an example of a tier two behavior plan that was used on several third grade boys in an urban elementary school. There is a single behavior and it was developed as a tier two intervention. There were three other students included on this plan.

Table 2.1: Tier Two Plan. Source: Author.

Targeted Behaviors	*Function of Behavior*
Disruptive behaviors disturbing the learning of others	A mal-adaptation of behavior when frustrated. Lack of skills. Seen as a "can't" behavior.

Students are displaying behaviors that disrupt the learning of the other students in the class. The hypothesis is that they are choosing these behaviors because they do not have mastery or knowledge of appropriate replacement behaviors. As a result, the following plan was developed:

1) Students will participate in a Skillstreaming class to identify and practice alternatives to the disruptive behaviors.
2) Students will use the replacement behaviors in appropriate situations. If they utilize these new behaviors, they will earn 5 bonus bucks used for spending at the end of the day.
3) Each week the number of times student can make an inappropriate choice in these situations will be reduced by two. Also, the number of teacher-initiated reinforcements or cues will decrease from several per day to one or less per day by week 6.
   week #1—10 times
   week #2—8 times
   week #3—6 times

week #4—4 Times
week #5—2 times
week #6—0 times

4) Each day the group will meet with intervention specialist, teacher, or school psychologist to discuss the day's events, tally the scores, and discuss alternatives to mistaken behaviors.

This looked like a fairly well-developed tier two intervention. As it was implemented the behaviors of these students improved slightly for the first week. During the second week it began to fail. The classroom teacher told the IAT that the Skillstreaming (McGinnis & Goldstein, 1997) training was not happening because of the lack of time. The school psychologist was unable to assist with the training and it didn't happen. Also the classroom teacher expressed frustration at being unable to keep track of the number of times she offered verbal reinforcement during the day stating, "I have too many other things going on." By the third week the teacher came back to IAT and explained that because there were 25 other students in the class whose learning was being disrupted because of these students she could no longer implement the plan. The pressures on this teacher were tremendous. The reality of the situation was that she had five students on a tier two behavioral intervention plan, 10 students whose instruction was differentiated, which required her to plan additional lessons for them, one identified special education student manifesting severe learning disabilities who was requiring specially designed instruction, and the remainder of the class who were identified as tier one students who were identified as "typically" developing. All of the students were required to pass the district standardized test. The school was already on the "watch list" by the state so the testing pressure was great. The IAT agreed and moved these students to tier three. Each had an individual behavior plan now, to be measured and implemented by the classroom teacher. The nature of the plans moved from an instructive tone and target to a purely behavioral one. All the plans developed were based upon specific behaviors (silence, head down when frustrated). The tier three plan is below:

Table 2.2: Tier Three Plan. Source: Author.

Targeted Behavior	Function of Behavior
Disruptive behaviors disturbing the learning of others	A mal-adaptation of behavior when frustrated. Seen as a "won't" behavior

Students are displaying behaviors that disrupt the learning of the other students in the class. The hypothesis is that they are choosing these behaviors because they do not have mastery or knowledge of appropriate replacement behaviors. As a result the following plan was developed:

1) Students will use the replacement behaviors in appropriate situations. If they utilize these new behaviors, they will earn 5 bonus bucks used for spending at the end of the day.

2) Each week the number of times student can make an inappropriate choice in these situations will be reduced by two. Also, the number of teacher-initiated reinforcements or cues will decrease from several per day to one or less per day by week 6.

3) When the student meets target behaviors they will be rewarded 10 bonus bucks:
   week #1—10 times
   week #2—8 times
   week #3—6 times
   week #4—4 times
   week #5—2 times
   week #6—0 times

4) Each day the classroom teacher will meet with each student to look at record sheet and provide rewards for met behavior.

The changes in the plan are subtle but noticeable. The tone of the plan has changed from one that was targeting behaviors that the teacher and the team saw as "can't" behaviors because of the lack of critical social skills to a plan that now considers the student behavior as a "won't" behavior. In other words, the student has the skills but is choosing not to comply. It has moved from an issue of skill deficit to noncompliance. This is a common tendency. With these tonal changes there is also a refocusing of viewing behavioral issues as a "within" child problem that needs to be fixed quickly or the child removed. The plan has also moved to a strictly behavioral proposition. "If" you comply, "Then" you will earn the reward.

Fading behaviors, highly structured plans with intricate reward systems, end up being reduced to what I call a "behavioral common denominator." "If" you do this, "Then" you get this. This is because of the pressures of the testing culture, too many kids on too many plans, and the inherent and pressing need for the teacher to have order and obedience so she can cover the required information. This is not a recipe for behavior change or autonomy, and these issues are only compounded when the behaviors are more severe and the contextual pressures on teachers and students are greater.

The disconnect between what well-meaning researchers vision as a viable PBIS program and what really occurs is caused by the fact that the researchers are generally not and have never been classroom teachers. They have no contextual understanding of the complexity of the classroom environment or the severity of the pressures teachers operate under. Likewise, the designers of all of the various flavors of PBIS are generally white, middle class and they cannot help but bring their bias with them in their findings. Lastly, most of the teachers and facilitators of the IAT and PBIS models are white, middle class, and women. The bias of this single perspective is well documented and skews the findings of the often quoted "research-based techniques" used in controlling student behavior (Bornstein, 2017). The effects of this bias combined with the ineffectiveness of the behavioral techniques described earlier are what I believe are the culprits in the overidentification of poor, black, and underrepresented children. The outcomes are very easy to document and easily traced to these systemic problems.

When we deconstruct the assessments and research that is used to legitimize PBIS we see some serious flaws. First, the predominance of the research uses the ODR as the measure of success or failure. If an intervention decreases the number of office referrals, then the intervention is seen as a success and the intervention receives the stamp of approval as a "research-based technique." However, we have seen that simply preventing the child from being sent to the office does not necessarily show that the student has engaged in learning or even stopped the identified behavior. It may mean that the teacher just has not sent him to the office (Harry & Klingner, 2014). Secondly, most methods of data collection during intervention are inconsistent at best and sloppy at worst. Collecting data, while you are teaching, while you are collecting academic and formative data, is not easily done. I believe it results in reducing a very complex behavioral, emotional, and cognitive issue into a "behavioral common denominator"; "If" you do this, you will "get" this.

Fundamental Attribution Error

FAE is defined by Harman (1999) as the error of ignoring situational factors and overconfidently assuming that the distinctive behaviors are due to an agent's distinctive character traits. This error motivates behavior planning that looks at internal states rather than considering external or contextual variables. This error fundamentally changes the nature of all interventions. The behavior issues being addressed are attributed to something within the child that changes the tone and tenor of the intervention design. This type of environment applies pressure on teachers and administrators to encourage obedience and compliance of students because it serves the greater good of the testing culture. It is also inclined to blame the student for the behavior problems they manifest in lieu of contextual or even teacher-created variables. It creates a culture that is looking to fix or segregate students. In this milieu children manifesting behavioral issues are the least tolerated and the ones most likely to be rushed through the intervention process. If you are poor, African-American, or an otherwise underrepresented minority, you are 2.28 times more likely to be identified with the medicalized label of Emotional Disturbance or Intellectually Disabled and are 2.75 times more likely to be segregated and placed in a self-contained classroom as were all other ethnic groups combined (Harry & Klingner, 2014). Schools are motivated to place these students away from typically developing peers and away from those that they might disturb.

The cost of the FAE is that teachers often inaccurately identify nonexistent internal pathology in students before they identify external variables in the environment or even teacher-caused problems. This results in inaccuracies in the targeting and developing of behavioral intervention plans, failure of the plans, and an accelerated identification process in special education. These consequences seem to affect African-American males at a higher rate than others. It has been well documented that these types of identifications early on in the school careers can have deterministic results for children (Bornstein, 2017). They are identified as "severely emotionally disturbed" or otherwise defective and are put on a track of disability that is very difficult if not impossible to get off of (Sullivan and Sadeh, 2014). Identification with a disability label legally lasts for three years and has been shown to emotionally last a lifetime (Bogdan & Taylor, 1982).

Conclusion

Does behaviorism work at all? Is there any use for this antiquated way of viewing and understanding human behavior? The research is pretty clear on this point. Bribes or "If"/"Then" propositions work for a very limited number of situations. Broadly speaking this type of bribe works for short periods of time if the goal of the bribe is to merely control the person (Kohn, 1999).

If, for example, you are substitute teaching and you set up a series of bribes to control the class while you are there. There are no relationships to worry about because you will be gone after a day and you need only control the behavior of the class while you are there. Changing behavior is not your concern. It also seems to work for short periods of time when the task is uninteresting or dull (Deci et al., 2001). Short time intervals reduce the issue of "hedonic adaptation." Aside from these situations it does not work to change behavior; in fact it might make things worse. What is needed is an ecological perspective that understands the importance of community support, of friendships and interaction and the valuing of an internal locus of control (Pink, 2009). ABA-guided intervention plans that place the sole focus on eliminating or extinguishing targeted behaviors will fail because of the lack of contextual understanding, attribution errors, and the overall emphasis of stopping the behavior rather than changing it. Even if they do work for short periods of time there are negative effects of this type of plan and will reduce interest in the task and erode achievement as well (Lepper et al., 1973).

References

Alberto, P., & Troutman, A. (2006). *Applied behavioral analysis for teachers* (7th ed.). New York, NY: Prentice Hall.

Amabile, T. M. (1993). Motivational synergy: Toward new conceptualizations of intrinsic and extrinsic motivation in the workplace. *Human Resource Management Review, 3*(3), 185–201.

Amabile, T. M., Hennessey, B. A., & Grossman, B. S. (1986). Social influences on creativity: The effects of contracted-for reward. *Journal of Personality and Social Psychology, 50*(1), 14–23.

Ames, C. (1978). Children's achievement attributions and self-reinforcement: Effects of self-concept and competitive reward structure. *Journal of Educational Psychology, 70*(3), 345.

Ariely, D., Gneezy, U., Lowenstein, G., & Mazar, N. (2005). *Large studies and big mistakes*. Federal Reserve Bank of Boston Working Paper No. 05–11.

Baglieri, S. (2008) "I connected": reflection and biography in teacher learning toward inclusion.' *International Journal of Inclusive Education, 12* (5–6), pp. 585–604 .

Bogdan, R. B., & Taylor, S. A. (1982). *Inside out. The social meaning of mental retardation.* Toronto, ON: University of Toronto Press.

Boggiano, A. K., Shields, A., Barrett, M., Kellam, T., Thompson, E., Simons, J., & Katz, P. (1992). Helplessness deficits in students: The role of motivational orientation. *Motivation and Emotion, 16*, 271–296.

Bornstein, J. (2017). Can PBIS build justice rather than merely restore order? In *The school to prison pipeline: The role of culture and discipline in school* (pp. 135–167). Bingley, UK: Emerald Publishing Limited.

Brickman, P., & Campbell, D. T. (1981). Hedonic relativism and planning the good society. In M. Appley (Ed.), *Adaptation-level theory* (pp. 287–305). New York, NY: Academic Press.

Campbell, A. (1981). *A sense of well-being in America: Recent patterns and trends.* New York, NY: McGraw Hill.

Charney, R. S. (1998). *Teaching children to care: Management in the responsive classroom.* Greenfield, MA: Northeast Foundation for Children.

Condry, J. (1977). Enemies of exploration: Self-initiated versus other-initiated learning. *Journal of Personality and Social Psychology, 35*(7), 459–477.

Covey, S. (1987). *The seven habits of highly effective people.* New York, NY: Simon & Schuster.

Deci, E. L. (1971). Effects of externally mediated rewards on intrinsic motivation. *Journal of personality and Social Psychology, 18*(1), 105.

Deci, E. L., Koestner, R., & Ryan, R. (2001). Extrinsic rewards and intrinsic motivation in education: Reconsidered once again. *Review of Educational Research, 71*, 1–27.

Deci, E. L., & Ryan, R. M. (2008). Facilitating optimal motivation and psychological well-being across life's domains. *Canadian Psychology/Psychologie canadienne, 49*(1), 14.

Deming, W. E. (1986). *Out of the crisis.* Cambridge, MA: Massachusetts Institute of Technology, Center for Advanced Engineering Study.

Elliot, S. N., McKevitt, B. C., & DiPerna, J. C. (2002). Promoting social skills and development of socially supportive learning environments. In S. E. Brock, P. J. Lazarus, & S. R. Jimerson (Eds.), *Best Practices in school crisis prevention and intervention* (pp. 151–170). Bethesda: National Association of School Psychologists.

Erikson, E. H. (1953). Growth and crises of the healthy personality. In C. Kluckhohn, H. A. Murray, & D. Schneider (Eds.), *Personality in nature, society, and culture* (2nd ed., pp. 185–225). New York, NY: Knopf.

Eysenck, S. B. J., & Eysenck, H. J. (1975). *Manual of the Eysenck personality questionnaire.* London: Hodder & Stoughton.

Fletcher, J. M., Coulter, W. A., Reschly, D. J., & Vaughn, S. (2004). Alternative approaches to the definition and identification of learning disabilities: Some questions and answers. *Annals of Dyslexia, 54*(2), 304–331.

Foucault, M. (1977). *Discipline and punish: The birth of the prison.* New York, NY: Pantheon Books.

Foucault, M. (1988). *Madness and civilization: A history of insanity in the age of reason.* New York, NY: Vintage, Random House.

Frederick, S., & Loewenstein, G. (1991). Do workers prefer increasing wage profiles? *Journal of Labor and Economics, 9*, 67–84.

Frederick, S., & Loewenstein, G. (1999). Hedonic adaptation. In D. Kahneman, E. Diener, & N. Schwarz (Eds.), *Well being. The foundations of hedonic psychology* (pp. 302–329). New York, NY: Russell Sage Foundation.

Freire, P. (1990). *Pedagogy of the oppressed.* New York, NY: Continuum.

Freire, P. (1998). *Pedagogy of freedom.* Lanham, MD: Rowman & Littlefield Publishers.

Gartrell, D. (2002). Replacing time-out: Part two—Using guidance to maintain an encouraging classroom. *Young Children, 57*(2), 36–43.

Glucksberg, S. (1962). The influence of strength of drive on functional fixedness and perceptual recognition. *Journal of Experimental Psychology, 63*(1), 36–41.

Goldstein, H., Sprafkin, R., Gershaw, N., & Klein, P. (1980). *Skillstreaming the adolescent: A structured learning approach to teaching pro-social skills.* Champaign, IL: Research Press.

Harman, G. (1999). Moral philosophy meets social psychology: Virtue ethics and the fundamental attribution error. In *Proceedings of the Aristotelian society* (pp. 315–331). Aristotelian Society. Vol.99, Oxford, UK: Oxfoprd University Press.

Harry, B., & Klingner, J. (2014). *Why are so many minority students in special education?* New York, NY: Teachers College Press.

Kami, C. (1989). *Young children continue to reinvent arithmetic.* New York, NY: Teachers College Press.

Kavale, K. (1990). 'Differential programming in serving handicapped students'. In: Wang, M. C., Reynolds, M. and Wahlberg, H. J. (Eds) Special Education: Research and Practice. Oxford: Pergamon Press, pp. 35–55

Klingner, J. K., & Bianco, M. (2006). What is special about special education for culturally and linguistically diverse students with disabilities? In B. Cook & B. Schirmer (Eds.), What is special about special education? (pp. 37–53). Austin, TX: Pro-Ed

Kohn, A. (1992). *No contest: The case against competition.* New York, NY: Houghton Mifflin Harcourt.

Kohn (1995) Teaching children to care. Video series, Choosing Community. Oakland, CA: Developmental Studies Center

Kohn, A. (1999). *Punished by rewards: The trouble with gold stars, incentive plans, A's, praise, and other bribes.* New York, NY: Houghton Mifflin Harcourt.

Koob, G. F., Stinus, L., Le Moal, M., & Bloom, F. E. (1989). Opponent process theory of motivation: Neurobiological evidence from studies of opiate dependence. *Neuroscience Biobehavioral Reviews, 13,* 135–140.

Krezmien, M. P., Leone, P. E., & Achilles, G. M. (2006). Suspension, race, and disability: Analysis of statewide practices and reporting. *Journal of Emotional and Behavioral Disorders, 14*(4), 217–226.

Lee, J. S. (2012). The effects of the teacher–student relationship and academic press on student engagement and academic performance. *International Journal of Educational Research, 53,* 330–340.

Lee, A., Wood, A. L., & Browder, D. M. (2015). Systematic instruction. In F. Brown, J. Anderson, & R. L. DePry (Eds.), *Individual positive behavioral supports* (pp. 221–235). Baltimore, MD: Brookes Publishing.

Lepper, M. R., Greene, D., & Nisbett, R. E. (1973). Undermining children's intrinsic interest with extrinsic reward: A test of the "overjustification" hypothesis. *Journal of Personality and Social Psychology, 28*(1), 129–137.

Libbey, H. P. (2004). Measuring student relationships to school: Attachment, bonding, connectedness, and engagement. *Journal of School Health, 74*(7), 274–283.

McCullers, J., Fabes, R., & Moran Ill, J. (1987). Does intrinsic motivation theory explain the adverse effects of rewards on immediate task performance? *Journal of Personality and Social Psychology, 52*(5), 1027–1033.

McGinnis, E., & Goldstein, A. P. (1997). Skillstreaming the elementary school child. Champaign, IL: Research Press.

Miller, L. B., & Estes, B. W. (1961). Monetary reward and motivation in discrimination learning. *Journal of Experimental Psychology, 61*(6), 501–504.

Piaget, J. (1965). *The moral judgment of the child*. New York, NY: Free Press. (Originally published 1938).

Piaget, J. (1973). *To understand is to invent*. New York, NY: Grossman. (Originally published 1948).

Pink, D. H. (2009). *Drive: The surprising truth about what motivates us*. New York, NY: Penguin.

Pugach, M. & Johnson, L. (1995) Collaboration as specific problem solving, in *Collaborative Practitioners, Collaborative Schools*. Denver, Love Publishing Company

Riffel, L. (2007). *Writing behavioral Intervention plans based on functional behavioral assessments: Making data based decisions*. Retrieved October 1, 2017 from www.behaviordoctor.org

Scheerer, M., Maddux, J. E., & Mercandante, B. (1982). The self efficacy scale: Constructing validation. *Psychological Reports, 51*(2), 663–671.

Sciovsky, T. (1976). The joyless economy: The psychology of human satisfaction. New York: Oxford University Press.

Skiba, R., Simmons, A., Ritter, S., Kohler, K., Henderson, M., & Wu, T. (2006). The context of minority disproportionality: Practitioner perspectives on special education referral. *Teachers College Record, 108*(7), 1424.

Spence, J. (1970). The distracting effects of material reinforcers in the discrimination learning of lower- and middle-class children. *Child Development, 41*(1), 103–111.

Spence, J. (1971). Do material rewards enhance the performance of lower-class children? *Child Development, 42*(5), 1461–1470.

Sullivan, A. L., & Sadeh, S. S. (2014). Differentiating social maladjustment from emotional disturbance: An analysis of case law. *School Psychology Review, 43*, 250–271.

Ursavaş, O. F., & dan Reisoglu, I. (2017). The effects of cognitive style on Edmodo users' behavior. A structural equation modeling-based multi-group analysis. *The International Journal of Information and Learning Technology, 34*(1), 31–50.

Viesti, C. R. Jr. (1971). Effect of monetary rewards on an insight learning task. *Psychonomic Science, 23*, 181–183.

Vygotsky, L. (1978). Interaction between learning and development. *Readings on the Development of Children, 23*(3), 34–41.

Zedlow, P. B. (1976). Some anti-therapeutic effects of the token economy: A case in point. *Psychiatry, 39*, 318–324.

Zubin, J. (1932). *Some effects of incentives*. New York, NY: Teachers College.

· 3 ·

THE ULTIMATE GOAL

Autonomy, Inner Locus of Control

Social Justice Issues for Chapter Three:

1. *Positive Behavioral Intervention Supports rob children of their social capital and power.*
2. *Positive Behavioral Intervention Supports keep underrepresented children down in an unequal relationship with authority.*
3. *Systemic and structural realities maintain unequal power relationships and maintain the "Status Quo."*

The purpose of this chapter is to describe the fundamental building blocks of an inner locus of control. This is the ability to make autonomous choices based upon an internal process rather than threats of punishment or promises of rewards. Comer (2015) calls the acquisition of this ability "social capital." This indicates that the ability to guide one's own behavior has social value and can serve as currency within a social context and proved power to the individual. Several researchers have investigated these individual building blocks and have called them by different names, but they are ultimately the same things. They are: schema development and a constructivist understanding of learning, language, and language development in the scaffolding of new behaviors; positive social climate and positive supportive relationships; and the development of autonomy. These are what Comer sees as the pieces of social capital necessary in the attainment of knowledge and the acquisition of skills, allowing students to choose behaviors. Researchers call this an inner locus of control, and its development is mutually exclusive of behaviorally oriented intervention strategies (Kamii, 1989; Piaget, 1965). These will be deconstructed by first looking at the way in which theorist have described the value of approaching learning from an experiential or process-driven perspective. A constructivist approach that relies upon the scaffolding of learning by adults and more sophisticated learners fits perfectly in a discussion about developing an internal locus of control. Second, the importance of new language development will be discussed. Vygotsky (1978) elaborated on the fact that with all new learning new language must also develop. Last, the importance of several socioemotional-based concepts will be peeled back. These concepts include the centrality of relationships to all learning as well as broader socioemotional developmental issues like the development of intellectual as well as moral and emotional autonomy (Seligman, Ernst, Gillham, Reivich, & Linkins, 2009). The chapter will conclude with a description of existing classroom frameworks that meet the criteria of schema and language development, and social emotional learning requirements that are deconstructed in the chapter. They will serve as preliminary templates for the presentation of a more socially just and autonomy-centered intervention approach.

Importance of a Constructivist Perspective: Language and an Internal Locus of Control

A schema is a framework of understanding that is formed during the process of learning (Levine & Munsch, 2014). Piaget developed the idea that learning is a constructive process that is based upon previous learning. As a child learns, they assimilate and accommodate new information using the existing frameworks they have formed (Levine & Munsch, 2014). As experiences happen and new information is presented, new schemas are developed and old schemas are changed or modified. While this theory is widely used in the explanation of acquiring and organizing academic knowledge it can also be used to describe and explain the process of learning new behaviors. Rather than the behaviorist view this way of constructing understanding is based upon an internal process of learning, reflecting, talking about, and eventually changing behaviors guided by the individual themselves and supported by the responsive group of peers who scaffold the learning (Lindon & Brodie, 2016).

Schemas can be very rigid and slow to change. Piaget believed that it is only through experience and the process of reflection on that new learning that adapted schemas can be formed. Vygotsky (1978) would add that the process of constructing an understanding of individual behavior can only happen in the presence of others. Through interaction, discussion, reasons, and justifications for new behaviors become apparent and because the individual thinks out loud and realizes the appropriate choice because of this thinking and exchange of ideas he makes his own choice (Kamii, 1989).

This alternative view of developing an internal locus of control is crucial to understanding the injustice present in the current PBIS models and in particular an ABA approach. In a Piagetian, constructivist model it is the process of learning that is crucial and seen as the key to eventual change. This is seen as an internal and personal process that is always happening. An ABA approach values the product of positive or negative reinforcement. In fact, the product is all that matters. The goal is to stop the behavior, or to elicit a new behavior. But these interactions are dependent upon external forces acting upon the child. If, as we have described in previous chapters, that external force is acting with inherent bias of some kind then the reinforcement, and the new behaviors being elicited, may produce negative cultural outcomes. This "control" has been shown to affect students from underrepresented minority groups more dramatically than other groups.

Vygotsky (1978) stated, "Education restructures all of the child's mental functions" (p. 38). He also agreed with Piaget that schooling, in general, provided only a narrow skill, such as learning to add or subtract, whereas instruction that includes new ways of thinking contributes to a broader schema and framework of understanding. In this way his conception of deep learning is very similar to Piaget's concept of schema development. The difference is that Piaget saw this type of learning as largely individual, whereas Vygotsky sees that interaction with adults and more competent peers as the only way to achieve deep learning and internalization of concepts (Trawick-Smith, 2017). The internal transformations that build toward advanced thinking are dialectical, not incremental. They are also heavily contextual. Vygotsky (1981) found that "The outcomes of cognitive development are not simply a continuation of elementary functions and are not their mechanical combination, but a qualitatively new mental formation" (p. 35), resulting in a personal and contextual justification and motivation to learn and use this new behavior.

The efficacy of this perspective stands in contrast to the controlling and limited view offered by a behavioral perspective. An internal change model like the ones described by Vygotsky and Piaget provides a view of a liberating process guided by internal choices and construction of understanding, while the ABA approach manipulates the individual to seek the rewards of showing the desired behavior that someone else deems as appropriate. One is freeing, the other controlling or, to use language from Chapter two, ABA encourages heteronomy and Piaget/Vygotsky encourage autonomy.

Sharing a common language when discussing behavioral issues with students is also a positive outcome of a more constructivist approach. Prochaska (1994) found that using language-based exercises was useful in encouraging positive growth within the trans-theoretical behavior change model. A common language to scaffold discussions and reflections on personal behaviors would aid in the changing of those behaviors. A language-based view of behavioral change that results in an internal locus of control is based in what Vygotsky (1981) referred to as an aggregate of acts of judgment, apperception, interpretation, and recognition united within a particular psychological structure. New learning always occurring within a responsive, supportive, reflective, and instructive environment (Charney, 1998).

Vygotsky (1978) spoke of the link between language development and learning. The learning of new information or the accommodation of new information is inextricably linked to new language development. Even in infants the nonverbal or inner language is considered important to the formation of new ways of thinking. It is also necessary for the internalization of new behaviors (Vygotsky, 1981). In fact, without the development of language around new behaviors, new learning would be very difficult if not impossible. The act of scaffolding is language based as well. The support that an adult or more competent peer provides in the mastery of new learning is dependent upon effective use of language. Vygotsky found that learning could not occur unless this dyadic relationship, based in language, was present.

If we take, for example, a typical behaviorally focused interaction between a teacher and student there is very little exchange of language. The student is cued as to the behavior and told the negative consequences if he continues to behave in that manner. The student chooses. The teacher administers the positive or negative reinforcement and the behavior is controlled or the consequence is administered. There is no discussion as to why the behavior is required, or what was inappropriate about the behavior. The student was not involved with the development of the rules or the consequences. In a classroom that emphasizes the development of language around the learning of new behaviors a discussion would have taken place and the student would have been involved in the creation of the rules and desired behaviors.

Discussions would have occurred as to why the behavior is desired and why the student would benefit from that chosen behavior. All of this combined with a classroom where children are engaged in learning and feel that they are an accepted member of the larger group there will be fewer behavioral issues. The child is aware of the required behavior, a reason for that behavior, and feels a part of the development of the rule. All of this requires language.

The Importance of Positive Relationships in the School

Dr. James Comer and his colleagues worked in, what were at the time, the two lowest performing elementary schools in Connecticut. His school development program is a research-based, comprehensive K–12 reform program grounded in the principles of child development. There is a famous quote that is attributed to him that speaks to the importance of positive relationships and how they affect learning. "There is no significant learning without significant relationships" (Payne, 1996, p. 9). Fundamental to his reform program is the importance of trusting, nurturing, and caring environments for children. He and his fellow researchers have found that the trust and collaborative environment that positive school cultures create proactively help students engage in learning and socially positive choices with their behaviors (Comer, 2010).

The key to engagement and, hence, fewer behavioral issues is not what we do "to" kids, it is what we do "with" them (Kohn, 1995). Resiliency research has long stated the importance of having at least one positive relationship to ensure resiliency in children (Werner, 2005). Often that one relationship is at school and is a function of the classroom environment the child exists in (Werner, 2005). Often a teacher or another student will be the "life buoy" for students who are struggling behaviorally. Wheatley (1994) stated the importance of relationships using a scientific metaphor. It also speaks to the importance of doing away with inadequate mechanical models like ABA to explain things:

> The Newtonian model of the world is characterized by materialism and reductionism—a focus on things rather than relationships. The quantum view of reality strikes against most of our notions of reality. Even to scientists, it is admittedly bizarre. But it is a world where relationship is the key determiner of what is observed and of how particles manifest themselves. Many scientists work with the concept of fields, invisible forces that structure space and behavior. (pp. 8–13)

Comer (2015) found that a supportive school culture that emphasizes relationships and language development also develops what he sees as the crucial element in schools today, Social Capital. He defines Social Capital as:

> The relationships, norms and trust acquired in meaningful networks that provide individuals and groups with the capacities to gain the training and tools necessary to participate in the economic and related mainstream networks of our society. Such participation provides productive and economic benefits to individuals; and/or social and human capital for the society. (p. 256)

In our society that moves information instantly, has rapid physical mobility, and also manifests fractured social networks, the skills that assist children in acquiring social capital are less predictably taught at home. The result of this is less social cohesion and unclear social expectations. To function effectively in this ever-changing environment there needs to be an acquisition of social capital that is able to afford students with the skills to cope (Carnoy, 2000; Reich, 1991). This acquisition is not occurring in many of our schools and a behaviorally influenced PBIS works directly against the development of social capital. The emphasis of standardized curriculum and a hyper-focus on achievement as measured by standardized tests has created an educational environment that devalues the development of social capital, encourages PBIS structures that value controlling behaviors, promotes obedience and conformity, and ultimately leaves the student unable to internally mange his/her own self (Leibbrand & Watson, 2010).

Covey (1987) uses another metaphor to illustrate the importance of relationships when he talks about the development of trust. In a teacher–student relationship each interaction has the potential to build or diminish trust. He uses the "emotional bank account" as a metaphor. With each trustworthy interaction, a child experiences with an adult an emotional deposit is made. If there is an accumulation of these deposits a high level of trust is built. With high levels of trust, we see engagement and internal locus of control as outcomes (Covey, 1987). Withdraws can be made as well. This occurs when the student experiences a nontrustworthy behavior. A small emotional bank account balance manifests a low level of trust and defensiveness. This is when students will often engage in acting out behavior because of the defensiveness and lack of trust.

The development of trust occurs through a consistent and predictable relationship. It requires language and the give and take of communication. Behaviorally based practices often result in a lack of trust and, hence, a small or overdrawn emotional bank account because of the deemphasis of language, conversation, and give and take. A school that manages behaviors and interventions from a behavioristic perspective and is more concerned about doing things to kids to ensure compliance will have a lower level of trust and higher incidence of behavioral problems (Comer, 2015).

The goals that were described earlier, such as trust, caring relationships, engagement all work toward a positive school culture and decrease acting out behaviors in students. ABA strategies often work against these outcomes (Charney, 1998). There are many strategies and frameworks that work toward the development of these desired outcomes and serve as a proactive management tool preventing behavioral problems, hence limiting the necessity for behavioral interventions. They don't involve bribes, contracts, or "If"/"Then" agreements.

Comer (2015) relates a situation where trust was developed between a teacher and a student:

> For example, a 4th grade student who had made much progress toward functioning well began showing signs that he was upset—angry, fighting. Just before Christmas recess he angrily knocked over his desk. In the control through punishment era he would have been sent to the principal for punishment. Acting from a support for growth perspective his teacher noted that he appeared upset and offered to help. He began to cry and explained that he was looking forward to his father coming home from prison on a pass for the Christmas holidays. For some reason the pass had been taken away. His teacher expressed an understanding of his feelings, and then helped him think about a response that was less harmful to him and his classmates. She helped him write a letter addressing both his father's and his own disappointment, and his anticipation of a visit later on.

> The incident strengthened the emotional tie between the student and the teacher, deepening his social capital, and enabled him to become even more available to the work and primary mission of the school—academic learning. The school and all of its activities became a more positive and helpful place for him. Each experience of support helps students acquire a sense of being valued and belonging that in a usually good environment builds to an increased capacity to learn; deepening human development. Distrust between home and school among and between students, staff and parents are weakened and mainstream social capital is acquired by non-mainstream families. (p. 5)

This Emotional Bank Account deposit increased the "trust" balance between the teacher and the student and opened this relationship up to more trust and more risk from the student. It encouraged the development of social capital and skills in learning how to channel anger and frustration in less disruptive and more productive ways. Often in a behaviorally based classroom the "acting out" behavior would be simply met with a consequence and an immediate control of the situation. Many teachers still see this behaviorally expedient way of dealing with such behaviors as the most valuable way to maintain order and maximize achievement. However, "paying it forward" is seen by Comer (2015) as a way to avoid future disruptions and ensure a trusting relationship that fosters later deep learning.

Intellectual, Emotional, and Behavioral Autonomy

As discussed earlier Piaget (1965) and Kamii (1989) describe the primacy of developing autonomy in students. Kamii (1989) states its development as the "primary purpose of education" (pp. 46). Autonomy is the ability to make decisions, moral or intellectual, by considering relevant factors, independent of rewards and punishment. In a moral sense Kamii (1989) uses examples of Martin Luther King Jr. for moral autonomy. Even with the threat of great personal harm and harm to his family he still pursued the path to civil rights because of his steadfast moral autonomy and commitment to what he considered to be a morally correct path. Intellectual autonomy is the ability to make an intellectual decision, after considering all of the options, independent of rewards and punishment. Kamii (1989) uses the analogy of Copernicus to illustrate this point. He was autonomous and convinced of the truth of his theory that even when threatened with excommunication he held fast to what he knew was the truth. Intellectual autonomy also includes the ability to confidently explain or teach another person the intellectual concept they learned themselves. This will manifest itself in the classroom when students are asked to agree or disagree with an answer given in a math exercise. If you disagree you must explain why you disagree. This ability to confidently explain a concept displays intellectual autonomy. This is the goal of education (Kamii, 1989). It should also be the goal when teaching children appropriate ways to behave in school. We want students who choose to do the right thing and be able to explain why it was the right thing as opposed to a behavioral focus, which is only concerned with witnessing the approved behavior.

How is autonomy developed in students? Piaget (1965) would answer this question by saying that adults in the children's lives reinforce the child's natural heteronomy when they use rewards and punishment to elicit desired behaviors. This coercion hinders the development of autonomy and develops what Kohn (1995) calls "self-serving shrewdness." The exchange of points of view and open honest discussion during behavioral incidents in the classroom has been shown to encourage the development of schema that values honesty and openness (Kamii, 1989; Pink, 2011).

It must also be noted that punishment also works against the development of autonomy (Kelsey, 2010). Kamii (1989) describes three outcomes of punishment. The first is "calculation of risk," Children will calculate the risk of being caught. The second outcome of punishment is "blind obedience," This is the exact opposite of autonomy. The third and final outcome of punishment is "revolt." Revolt can take many forms in children's behavior from outright violence to passive aggressive behaviors. Acting out in this way is seen by many as a response to an environment that the child sees as punishing either directly as in being suspended from school or losing a privilege to indirectly as in coming into a school that the child feels that they are not welcomed, cared for, or safe. These behaviors have seen an increase in quantity and intensity in the past ten years (Bornstein, 2017). It is a well-established fact that children need a safe, caring, predictable environment for them to develop a healthy ego and sense of autonomy (Charney, 1998; Knestrict, 2006; Maslow & Lowery, 1998).

These are not new ideas. The expedience of behaviorally based PBIS strategies is hard to resist. When teachers and administrators are pressured to raise achievement and pace the curriculum in standardized fashion obedience looks pretty good. But it is at the expense of the child that we make this choice. While 85% of students in schools do not require anything more than tier one supports we tend not to worry about this much. However, if the dominant perspective is one of obedience and conformity even our tier one interventions within a PBIS model will reflect a behavioral focus and will devalue the interaction, language development, community building, and caring school environment necessary for the development of autonomy and an internal locus of control. The centrality of language development and autonomy is at the heart of these new ways of intervening on behaviors. We need not reinvent the wheel to change the current framework. Montessori education is a natural place to look first.

Montessori Method

Montessori (1974) spoke of the importance of developing both moral and intellectual autonomy. She focused her energy, however, on the classroom. She stated that people educated in this manner will be prepared to seek the truth

and make it an intimate part of their lives. Montessori felt that it was a fundamental purpose of school "to be charitable toward others and to cooperate with
them to make a better world for all" (p. 38). There is an emphasis of developing
autonomy that is embedded in all of the methods. Fundamentally her method
was designed to encourage children to work deeply, independently, and for
each child to develop a sense of internal locus of control (Lillard, 2007). Even
the academic learning was designed for autonomy and devalued the external
controls typical of most classrooms by using concepts like "control for error"
in which the student would check and defend their own work as opposed to
solely getting praise or rejection from the teacher. They use this self-feedback
to make adjustments in their work and then check it again.

Much of the Montessori curriculum is self-guided. Students have far more
choice in what they do and how they do it. This self-direction has been linked
to fewer behavioral issues in the classroom as well as a greater internal sense of
autonomy, efficacy, and the development of an internal locus of control (Blake
Schwartz, 2017). Studies have also found that students in Montessori classrooms tended to display better abilities on social and behavioral assessments,
demonstrating a greater sense of justice and fairness. On the playground they
were much more likely to engage in emotionally positive play with peers and
less likely to engage in aggressive play (Lillard, 2007).

Lillard (2007) identifies eight principles of Montessori method all of
which can be seen as proactive management techniques as well as methods
of developing an internal locus of control. When we look at these principles,
the emphasis put on language, communication, and autonomy is also obvious:

1. *Movement and Cognition*—movement and cognition are closely
   entwined. Movement is something that children need developmentally and can be seen as a proactive management strategy.
2. *Choice*—learning and well-being are improved when people have a
   sense of control over their lives. Free choice is encouraged as long as
   respect is maintained. Children can also choose to observe.
3. *Interest*—people learn more deeply when they are interested in what
   they are learning. When the child reaches elementary age they can
   begin choosing what and how they study.
4. *Extrinsic Rewards Are Avoided*—tying extrinsic rewards to an activity
   or task negatively impacts motivation to engage in that activity.
5. *Learning from and with Peers*—a principle that aligns with what we
   know about scaffolding (Vygotsky, 1978). Collaborative arrange-
   ments can be conducive to learning.

6. *Learning in Context*—learning situated in meaningful context is often deeper and richer than learning in abstract context.

7. *Teacher Ways/Interactions*—particular forms of adult interactions are associated with more optimal learning outcomes for children. Scaffolding.

8. *Order/Predictability*—order and predictability are beneficial to the development of schema. During the primary years this is external to the child. In later childhood it becomes internalized if they have experienced order/predictability.

A More Responsive Classroom

Another perspective that is very closely related to the Montessori method is the Responsive Classroom (RC). Proponents of the RC state that the method serves as both a way of thinking about teaching students and also serving as an "academic enabler." Rimm-Kaufman and Chiu (2007) found that use of the RC techniques in the classroom serves as both an academic enabler and an effective proactive management method. These methods can be seen as effective tier one supports that do not depend on behavioral strategies and focus on teaching new skills through modeling, discussion, and practice in real time. There are two characteristics that stand out when teachers intentionally form emotionally supportive classrooms. The first is the modeling of interactions the teacher has with others in school. A teacher once told me that kids hear about half of what we say to them but they see everything we do. The second intentional characteristic of RC practice is developing a positive student–teacher relationship. Greeting children at the door every morning, asking them about what they did the night before, telling them what you did the night before all work toward this goal (Seligman et al., 2009). Covey (1987) states that sharing and listening are huge deposits in children's emotional bank accounts and work toward building high levels of trust.

Methods such as morning meeting, academic choice, and interactive modeling serve as fundamental strategies in teaching students new behaviors through interaction, real-time practice, and warm, supportive classroom relationships. The morning meetings also create a place where the students learn to problem solve, resolve conflicts, and work on basic social skills, collaborative development of rules as well as academic choice within academic learning. Elliot et al,(2002) found that when using the morning meeting strategy students' social skills improved, while problem behaviors decreased.

In the RC method it is fundamental to allow the students to help develop the classroom rules or "norms." This is done through a very tedious process by which the teacher facilitates the development of 3–5 classroom rules based upon discussions with the students about what they want to experience and accomplish during the school year. After they generate these "hopes and dreams" they are told that in order to experience these things there needs to be norms that their community operates under. Through more discussions facilitated by the teacher the class agrees upon the rules and then signs a contract agreeing to live and help teach these norms to the community (Charney, 1998). There is greater ownership and "buy in" with students using this method. It feels like their classroom. This process takes time and energy at the beginning of the school year that many teachers are not inclined to sacrifice. Wong and Wong (2015) found that it takes the first six weeks of school to establish the rules, rituals, and routines in a classroom to help facilitate order. It also takes energy and patience from the teacher as well as the confidence that time spent developing this level of predictability and classroom culture "buy-in" is worth it. In each of these examples the centrality of the development of autonomy through language and cooperative interaction with peers and with adults teaches new behaviors instead of buying them with rewards or punishment. Coercion being sold as behavior change is a fundamental flaw in the current PBIS system. Taking the time to develop a healthy and supportive, autonomy-driven classroom culture takes time to develop, quite possibly in lieu of academic instructional time. This is not encouraged by the standards-driven curriculum when teacher and administrator's jobs are dependent upon test scores and instructional time is seen as too valuable to waste on these types of methods.

Conclusion

There are well-researched characteristics of teaching and management techniques that have been found to assist students in the development of an internal locus of control. They all are organized under the umbrella of social capital, which has been defined as:

> The relationships, norms and trust acquired in meaningful networks that provide individuals and groups with the capacities to gain the training and tools necessary to participate in the economic and related mainstream networks of our society. (Comer, 2015, p. 3)

The goal of developing autonomy and an inner locus of control is the acquisition of social capital that allows individuals function independent of promises of rewards or threats of punishment.

The first concept working toward this goal is to begin thinking about learning new behaviors from a constructivist perspective. Piaget spoke of schemas as the frameworks of understanding that individuals form when learning new things. These schemas then are used as references with all new learning and are modified or added on to, as new knowledge is uncovered. Thinking of learning new behaviors in this way allows you to see the importance of practicing the skills and then processing them so that they can be adapted and changed.

Central to schema formation is language. Vygotsky (1978) found that all new learning involves new language. The idea that new learning and schema formation and adaptation cannot happen without this language was central to his idea of scaffolding and the importance of the dyadic verbal relationship between teacher and learner. If a behavioral approach is used in a school, there is very little processing or talking about behaviors beyond the administering of rewards or consequences. The goal is to stop the behavior and the reward or punishment is all the communication that is needed. A more interactive or process-oriented approach that in fact elicits the interaction as a way of processing and internalizing the change is seen as the only way for behaviors to change.

Creating a positive social environment is also crucial to changing behavior and helping students develop an internal locus of control. The work of Comer (2015) and Covey (1987) supports this notion. Examples including the Montessori method and Responsive Classroom Technique have been shown to facilitate positive social environments and supportive nurturing classrooms that are fertile grounds for teaching children to manage their own behaviors so others do not have to.

In the end Piaget (1965) stated that the goal of all education is to create students who are autonomous and able to manage themselves both intellectually and behaviorally. It is the ability to become autonomous that frees you from the bonds of reward and punishment and the hegemony of controlling influences.

References

Blake Schwartz, T. D. (2017). *The effect of student-led conferencing at school and at home on goal-setting, goal-fulfillment, effort, achievement, intrinsic motivation, and satisfaction for Montessori lower elementary 3rd year students.* Masters of Arts in Education Action Research Papers 224. Retrieved from http://sophia.stkate.edu/maed/224

Bornstein, J. (2017). Can PBIS build justice rather than merely restore order? In *The school to prison pipeline: The role of culture and discipline in school* (pp. 135–167). Bingley, UK: Emerald Publishing Limited.

Carnoy, M. (2000). *Sustaining the new economy: Work, family, and community in the information age.* New York, NY: Russell Sage Foundation.

Charney, R. S. (1998). *Teaching children to care: Management in the responsive classroom.* Greenfield, MA: Northeast Foundation for Children.

Comer, J. (2010). The Yale child study center school development program. In J. Meece & J. Eccles (Eds.), *Handbook on schools, schooling, and human development* (pp. 419–433). New York, NY: Routledge.

Comer, J. P. (2015). Developing social capital in schools. *Society, 52*(3), 225–231.

Covey, S. (1987). *The seven habits of highly effective people.* New York: Simon and Schuster.

Elliot, S. N., McKevitt, B. C., & DiPerna, J. C. (2002). Promoting social skills and development of socially supportive learning environments. In *Best practices in school crisis prevention and intervention* (pp. 151–170).

Kamii, C. (1989). *Young children continue to reinvent arithmetic.* New York, NY: Teachers College Press.

Kelsey, J. (2010). The negative impact of rewards and ineffective praise on student motivation. *ESSAI, 8,* Article 24.

Knestrict, T. (2006). *Rules, rituals and routines program guide and study guide for learning.* Lake Zurich, IL: Learning Seed Publishing.

Kohn. (1995). Teaching children to care. Video Series.

Leibbrand, J. A., & Watson, B. H. (2010). *The road less traveled—How the developmental sciences can prepare educators to improve student achievement: Policy recommendations.* Retrieved from http://www.ncate.org/dotnetnuke/LinkClick.aspx?fileticket=gY3FtiptMSo%3D&tabid=706

Levine, L. E., & Munsch, J. (2014). *Child development.* Los Angeles, CA: Sage.

Lillard, A. (2007). *Montessori: The science behind the genius.* New York, NY: Oxford University Press.

Lindon, J., & Brodie, K. (2016). *Understanding child development 0–8 years, 4th edition: Linking theory and practice.* London: Hodder Education.

Maslow, A., & Lowery, R. (1998). *Towards a psychology of being* (3rd ed.). New York, NY: Wiley & Sons.

Montessori, M. (1974). *Education for a new world.* Chennai, India: Kalakshetra Press. (Original work published 1946).

Payne, R. K. (1996). *A framework for understanding poverty.* Highlands, TX: aha! Process Inc.

Piaget, J. (1965). *The moral judgement of the child.* New York, NY: Free Press. (Originally published 1932).

Payne R. K. (1996). *A Framework for Understanding Poverty.* Highlands, TX: aha! Process Inc.

Pink, D. H. (2011). *Drive: The surprising truth about what motivates us.* New York: Penguin.

Prochaska, J. O., Norcross, J. C., & DiClemente, C. C. (1994). *Changing for good*. New York: Morrow. Released in paperback by Avon, 1995.

Reich, R. (1991). *The work of nations: Preparing ourselves for 21st-century capitalism*. London: Simon and Schuster.

Rimm-Kaufman S. E., Fan Xitao, C. Y. Iris & Wenyi (2007). The Contribution of the *Responsive Classroom* Approach on Children's Academic Achievement: Results From a Three-Year Longitudinal Study. *Journal of School Psychology, 45*, 401–421.

Seligman, M. E. P., Ernst, R. M., Gillham, J., Reivich, K., & Linkins, M. (2009). Positive education. *Oxford Review of Education, 35*, 293–311.

Trawick-Smith, J. (2017). *Early childhood development: A multicultural perspective* (7th ed.). Upper Saddle River, NJ: Merrill/Prentice Hall.

Vygotsky, L. (1978). Interaction between learning and development. *Readings on the Development of Children, 23*(3), 34–41.

Vygotsky, L. S. (1981). The genesis of higher mental functions. In J. V. Wertsch (Ed.), *The concept of activity in Soviet psychology* (pp. 144–188). Armonk, NY: Sharpe.

Werner, E. E. (2005). What can we learn about resilience from large-scale longitudinal studies. In S. Goldstein & R. B. Brooks (Eds.), *Handbook of resilience in children* (pp. 91–106). New York, NY: Springer.

Wheatley, M. J. (1994). *Leadership and the new science: Learning about organization from an orderly universe*. San Francisco, CA: Berrett-Koehler.

Wong, H. K., & Wong, R. T. (2015). *The first days of school: How to be an effective teacher*. Sunnyvale, CA: Harry K. Wong.

· 4 ·

THE CONTEXT OF SCHOOL CULTURE AND THE PREVENTION OF BEHAVIORAL INTERNALIZATION

Social Justice Issues for Chapter Four:

1. *Money encourages the labeling, identifying of difference.*
2. *A standards-based curriculum and culture encourage an obedience model, which maintains the social order.*
3. *Pseudo-science supports the continued used of a "difference model."*
4. *Guarding against Fundamental Attribution Error.*

The present form of discourse represents patriarchal manifestations of power and determinism (Sloan-Cannella, 1997). The current PBIS model frames behavior in a simplistic way devaluing the complexities and the contexts that drive student behavior. It also marginalizes those not in the power class who are making the intervention decisions. When these constructions are imposed on all human beings, power relations are created that foster injustice, oppression, and regulation (Sloan-Cannella, 1997, p. 157).

Why is a nurturing and caring, autonomy-driven classroom so difficult to achieve in our schools? Why is our central method of intervening on chronic behaviors seemingly the exact opposite of what is needed? There are many contextual reasons for this reality. In an environment that emphasizes the covering of curriculum as opposed to the uncovering of understanding, encourages compliance and obedience over autonomy, and is more concerned with measurement, assessment, and pacing of curriculum than deep learning, is it any wonder that the current iteration of the PBIS model is now ubiquitous? Chapter Four examines how the structure and goals of schools often encourage the continued use of a product-driven PBIS approach that provides the illusion of a well-organized, nurturing environment but in reality is creating a student population addicted to external control. There are five variables discussed. They are: (1) The Separateness of Behavior; (2) The valuing of obedience and control; (3) Political pressures to maintain the hierarchy; (4) The belief in the efficacy of special education; (5) The heuristic nature of learning new behaviors.

The Separateness of Behavior

It is a fundamental truth of the current PBIS model that the affective and behavioral realm of a student's life in school is treated as separate from the cognitive and academic realm. This is evidenced in several ways. The most obvious is that we organize a school using this premise. There are separate academic subjects, even though the reality of life is an integrated experience. Behavior is treated as a separate set of skills. Even the way we teach pre-service teachers is segmented and behavior is often presented as a separate course for "behavior management" detached from methods courses. In a classroom or a school, management is constructed as separate and is often developed independent of the context of a classroom culture or ecosystem.

Even during behavior intervention planning teams spend very little time considering the ecological variables that might be influencing student behavior. Flannery and Fenning (2014) describe only the behavior and the fact that the student was referred to the office and do not uncover any data about the context of the behavior. In fact, the preponderance of PBIS research refers to office discipline referrals (ODRs) and never to the reasons for the chosen behaviors. It is fundamental to a new vision of PBIS that the context be considered and contextual analysis be central to the new framework.

Ecological Models and Fundamental Attribution Error

Central to a new vision of PBIS must be the utilization of an ecological order of operations in the development of behavioral interventions.

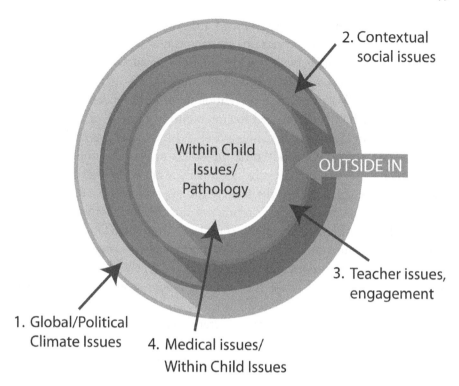

Figure 4.1 The Change Continuum. Source: Author.

Currently, intervention development often looks to the internal state of the child for explanations of the behaviors being chosen. This leads to a more behavioral way of developing interventions, encouraging the use of applied behavioral techniques. To guard against FAE a more ecological model should be used in a new intervention model. Bronfenbrenner and Morris (2006) offer a model that could be easily used to develop effective intervention plans and guard against FAE. The basic method would require an intervention team to work from the outside ecological environment toward the child. This would force teams to look at the external ecological variables before seeking internal states within the child. Figure 4.1 provides a visual of the model.

The Example of Travis

To illustrate how this might look an example of an intervention will be used that occurred in the development for this book. It took place in a large urban school district in Ohio. This school used a three-tiered intervention model. There was a well-established tier one system. Travis had shown little ability to control some of his behaviors with just tier one supports. Tier two and three were less well developed and typically students moved from tier one to what was essentially a tier-three intervention model. The student was a fourth grade male. He had been referred for intervention because of his constant disruptions in his late morning classes as well as his late day classes. Behaviors included not completing work, bothering others in class, talking out, and a slow but constant escalation of behavior usually resulting in temper outbursts and removal from class. When the team began to problem solve for this child they began by looking at the environments outside of school including the bus ride, the transitions into school, transitions from breakfast to the classroom, transitions and environment of the morning classes, and the afternoon transitions and expectations. They also considered teacher behavior, level of interest, and engagement of the lessons being taught as well as the management abilities of the teacher.

The team's initial conclusions were determined to be more environmental than internal to the child. The intervention plan that was developed targeted transitions and the types of work being presented in class. It was determined that Travis required a highly structured set of transitions and that a schedule for them would benefit his ability to follow them. Also, it was determined that Travis tended to escalate when he was hungry. So the autonomy to get a snack was provided for him. The intervention was initiated and was a success. The key to the process was the facilitation of an "outside in" intervention development process rather than an intervention targeting the child.

This is not to say that there won't be times that an intervention will need to be developed that targets internal states. The new model would dictate only looking for the "within child" characteristics last. This example will be looked at again in chapter five.

Valuing Obedience and Control

The most destructive outcome of an intervention model that emphasizes extrinsic motivation is that it creates an individual who craves extrinsic rewards. They are taught that the reason you do well in school is because of the rewards you earn (Kohn, 1999). Obedience and control are the desired outcomes of a behavioral approach. Unfortunately, mounting evidence shows that if you use external rewards to gain these you create a person who desires them all the more, hence the "Hedonic Adaptation" effect. Pink (2011) states:

> The opposite of autonomy is control. They sit at different poles of the behavioral compass. They point us toward different destinations. Control leads us to compliance; autonomy leads us to engagement. (pp. 108–109)

The larger point that is made is that engagement then leads to mastery. (Pink, 2011)

Pink (2011) describes that in the 20th century where much more of the work was routinized and repetitive it was required that work be done in a certain way, in a certain amount of time. It required workers to comply with the process that was dictated. This worked when the tasks were simple and repetitive. Simple rewards or threats of punishments were effective to gain compliance over the worker. The schools reflected this value by demanding conformity, compliance, and sameness (Coontz, 1992). For the tasks required of work in the 21st century these strategies will fall short. Solving complex problems collaboratively, within groups, requires engagement and the ability to think flexibly and has become a necessity in today's economy (Pink, 2011). Unfortunately, schools have not adjusted to these fundamental changes in the work world. This is reflected in education's emphasis on product-driven curriculum and assessment. This is seen in the antiquated way curriculum is divided and organized in schools currently. William (2011) likens today's work world to an escalator moving upward in increasing speed and complexity. If education is taught in discrete subject areas in the traditional way and measured through standardized tests then all students receive the same information at the same rate at the same time. When they enter the work world what they have learned in school will be obsolete within the first year of employment. The escalator passes them by. Making the ability to learn new things quickly and deeply is an important skill, but a skill set that is currently not taught using the curricular models that emphasize "Product" (discrete, measureable chunks of information) as opposed to "process," which is learning how to learn (Metacognition). Current achievement-based models encourage "product," leaving many students unengaged and unaware of how to learn new things quickly and deeply. The same is true with how we construct an understanding of teaching and learning new behavior. Students must learn not only the content of the new learning but also the codes and social skills required for that social milieu. Teaching students a fixed set of social skills or behavior is no longer enough. Like academic curriculum they need to learn the flexibility of code shifting and working collaboratively within groups (Charney, 1998). This can only be done in classrooms that emphasize the learning of "how to learn" and encourage intellectual and emotional autonomy.

The current behaviorally based PBIS models still emphasize compliance and obedience. They are product driven and are still in use because the curriculum requires obedience in order to be delivered so that all students can be measured in a standardized way. The economic drivers of the 20th century work world are still driving the behavioral management and intervention models well into the 21st century.

Heteronomy and Autonomy

The development of autonomy requires teaching in a way that deemphasizes the reward system and any externally driven motivation (Kamii, 1989). Heteronomy is the opposite of autonomy and is present when an individual is controlled by someone or something. A child who is controlled by a reward or threatened with punishment is heteronomous (Piaget, 1965). A more commonplace example of this would be the parent who offers rewards to their child for good grades. The implicit message that is sent by this interaction is that earning good grades does not have any intrinsic value, it requires payment. But it also implies that the person offering rewards is really in control of the person being bribed. PBIS, in fact most management strategies in schools today, are based in this type of externally driven reward system. What causes a person to become less autonomous and more heteronomous than others? Piaget (1965) answered this question by stating that adults reinforce children's natural heteronomy when they use rewards and punishment, thereby hindering the development of autonomy. Kamii (1989) gave a vivid example of what an alternative might look like by describing the following interaction:

> For example, if a child tells a lie, an adult can punish the child by depriving him of dessert. But the adult can also look at the child straight in the eye, with affection and skepticism say instead "I really can't believe what you are saying because (and give a reason). When you tell me something the next time I am not sure I'll be able to believe you, because I think you lied this time. I want you to go to your room and think about what happened". Children who are raised with this kind of exchange of viewpoints are likely, over time, to construct from within a value of honesty. An essential element in this equation is a warm human relationship of

natural respect and affection between the child and adult. If children believe that the adult does not care about them anyway they will have no reason to want to be believed. (p. 47)

The important difference to note here is that reasons were given for the behavior. Not a reward or a threat. This type of interaction requires language, patience, and time—three things that today's schools do not allow for. The entire curriculum is guided by pacing charts that dictate which standard is being taught on specific days. If a child falls behind, the pace of the class is never altered and the student is required to make up that ground. That type of thinking influences the pacing and the environment of the behavior management and intervention systems. Covering the curriculum is of utmost importance, often at the expense of the student uncovering a deep understanding of the material. Given the requirements of the paced curriculum it makes sense that management strategies and intervention systems adopt techniques that are quick, require little language and explanation, and terminate the behavior quickly so as to keep moving through the curriculum and on to the test! If your behavior gets in our way, we will bribe you or threaten you, either way the priorities are very clear. It must again be stated that these types of ways of thinking about behavior and PBIS have well-documented negative outcomes, especially for underrepresented students.

Political Pressures and Hierarchy

The political nature of education is well documented. In fact, some researchers claim that the entire educational system is subsumed by the market economy (Picciano & Spring, 2013). The political pressure to produce obedient, heteronomous workers is still strong and is the reason we have a paced, standardized curriculum and made the school culture test heavy. Data and test scores provide empirical but biased proof that students are learning and our tax dollars are being spent wisely. The schools merely reflect the greater culture (Hollins, 1996). The hierarchy that is constructed in the greater culture is mirrored in schools. Hierarchy is defined as a system of organization where individuals are ranked one above the other according to class, culture, gender, or status (Faris & Felmlee, 2014). Ranking occurs in several ways in schools although testing is one of the most powerful ways students are placed in the hierarchy. Socioeconomic sorting occurs too (Pickett & Wilkinson,

2015). Hair, Hanson, Wolfe, and Pollack (2015) reaffirmed the link between achievement and perceived school quality using socioeconomic status (SES) as the variable. The PBIS system often helps to recreate this hierarchy also by keeping children with significant cultural differences from advancing by using behavioral interventions as the tool (Bornstein, 2017). This hierarchy is also crucial to maintaining the educational industrial complex described by Picciano and Spring (2013) and also works to maintain the dominance of white middle-class leaders in education.

Capitalistic Models

McLaren (2015) writes that "public education today is in its death throes but refuses to acknowledge its own demise and its once proud luminaries fail to see how capitalism is responsible" (p. 2). The structure of schools and the systems that are used to function daily mirror those of our capitalistic society. This is mirrored in the PBIS system where the competencies are clearly defined to what the student will do to demonstrate learning for a workforce-related model. Obedience, heteronomy, compliance are at the core of what PBIS is trying to encourage. What McLaren (2015) states about education in general relates directly to PBIS and all empirically based assessments:

> They thrive in a world where the humanity of students is enslaved to a particular analytic structure combining instrumental reason, positivism and one directional objectivity. Its heteronomous dogma is all about increasing control over our external and internal nature, creating a reified consciousness in which the wounds of our youth are hidden behind the armor of scientificity. (p. 171)

These behavioral standards create a situation where the student who is experiencing behavioral difficulties must comply with the imposed standards of the culturally blind and capitalistically inspired norms which are demanded of him by a three-leveled PBIS model. This model does not reward behavioral and neurological diversity, and the justification is always that it is what the work world demands. However, because of the well-established bias of the behavioral expectations children who do not conform, or are seen by authority as unable or unwilling to conform, experience negative outcomes. These overwhelmingly are students of color or of low SES. These outcomes often have lifelong consequences (Bornstein, 2017; Gutierrez, 2006; Harry & Klingner, 2014).

Capitalism and the Efficacy of Special Education

Behavioral interventions that demand imposed behaviors on students and the Special Education Industrial Complex (SEIC) (Knestrict, 2017) are both supported by these capitalistic-driven concepts of compliance, obedience, and conformity. The tremendous amounts of money that support SEIC encourage a pathologizing of students. In terms of student behavior this means moving toward a label of Emotional Disturbance (a problematic label in itself). This fuels the engines of special education and maintains raw material for its processes and existence. Professors, teachers, school psychologists, experts, authors all have careers that depend on the maintenance of special education. It follows then that PBIS continues to feed the industry with raw materials that necessitate the framework and ensure the relevancy and the jobs of the people in the special education industrial complex. PBIS is merely a cog in the machine. Special Education has become a billion dollar economic venture and these people need to protect their investments. In terms of behavior and interventions the first step is pathologizing the behavior so that it is no longer a behavior problem but a "condition" that needs prescribed academic treatment. Usually this means a highly structured, behaviorally based externally driven management system. This label, severe emotional disturbance (SED), is the most problematic and easily manipulated label within IDEA. PBIS often encourages movement toward this label reinforcing the pseudo-scientific nature of special education and maintaining the industrial complex it is founded upon. It is job security! This is insidious and it negatively affects black and brown skinned males at a significantly higher rate to where some have called this the "school to prison pipeline" (Bornstein, 2017).

If we do away with the medicalization of special education, we erase the hierarchy it creates and by this action erase the capitalistic structures that encourage the current models. As was stated in previous chapters this belief in the efficacy of special education is not born of the research, and the belief in the legitimacy of special education labels fuels the belief in the inferiority of certain groups who seem to "have" these impairments in greater numbers. There is no escaping the stigma of these labels and the benefits of special education are still questionable at best (Kavale, 1990; Reschly, 1997). The fact that these issues affect, to a dramatic degree, students in underrepresented groups, and that failure of effectively remediating behavioral issues prior to special education placement may result in special education labeling, which is of questionable benefit, this issue becomes a social justice issue (Oakes, Lipton, Anderson, & Stillman, 2015).

The Heuristic Nature of Changing Behavior and Learning

In the worlds of capitalism and special education there is an ideology that communicates the importance of "product." In capitalism the product is at the root of all the theory professes. In special education and all education in general, product of learning is the possession of the knowledge that can be reflected on the test. This is as opposed to a valuing of "Process," which would assume that the process of learning to learn (metacognition) and constructing an understanding of the content is more valuable in the long run because it would enable the student to learn new things deeply. This valuing of "product" is reflected in education by the emphasis of testing and the devaluing of meta-cognition. Educational psychologists divide learning into two categories: algorithmic and heuristic. Algorithmic learning is one that is mapped out and the learner learns the steps to one conclusion. There is an algorithm or a formula to learning. Heuristic learning tasks are the opposite because there is no "one way" to solve the problem or learn the information. There are multiple possibilities and it requires creativity and flexibility of thinking (Pink, 2011). All authentic learning, at its core, is heuristic in nature. If passing a test is all that you need to worry about then this type of learning can be reduced to an algorithmic memorization. However, deep learning is a process that requires thinking, talking, processing, and practicing and we all arrive upon learning at different times in different ways. Pacing charts and standardized testing are not heuristic and encourage algorithmic thinking and learning, which was useful in the simpler times of the 20th century, but the new century requires more (Pink, 2011).

PBIS is an effort to make the learning of new behaviors and intrinsically monitoring your own behavior an algorithmic task. It is not. Mastering an intrinsic motivational self requires lots of practice; reflection, talking, role models, and we all learn these types of things in our own way, in our own time. Structuring the learning of social skills, for example, like you would an academic class, assumes that children will all learn at the same rate, experience the same practice, and master the same skills at the same time. Human skills require context and other humans to interact with (Charney, 1998. Autonomy requires learning through doing without the external control of someone dictating what is normal behavior and what is not. Both intellectual and emotional autonomy are mastered through doing. Learning in context in real time with opportunities to reflect, practice, discuss is essential to this type of learning and cannot be redesigned as an algorithmic task when at its core it is heuristic.

It is my contention that the teaching of an internal locus of control is mutually exclusive with standards-based, paced curriculum models. The culture and the schema that are used do not allow for the time and the context to adequately learn these skills in a genuine sense. It is also mutually exclusive of PBIS systems that are behavioristic in nature. If the goal of the management system is to control students for short periods of time and to create quiet and obedient children in an effort to elevate test scores and achievement in general, then these systems will do that. However, if your goal is to create a caring, self-paced, and supportive environment that is concerned with deep learning and developing caring kids with an internal locus of control, then a different more responsive classroom is required. A new design for PBIS is required. A model is required that is more responsive and caters to the heuristic needs of behavior change and the learning of new behaviors. The current PBIS model is far too algorithmic in nature and caters to the imposed norms that works toward control and not change; toward external rather than internal locus of control; and toward heteronomy rather than autonomy.

References

Bornstein, J. (2017). Can PBIS build justice rather than merely restore order? In *The school to prison pipeline: The role of culture and discipline in school* (pp. 135–167). Bingley, U.K.: Emerald Publishing Limited.

Bronfenbrenner, U., & Morris, P. A. (2006). The bio-ecological model of human development. In R. M. Lerner & W. Damon (Eds.), *Handbook of child psychology: Vol. 1. Theoretical models of human development* (6th ed., pp. 793–828). Hoboken, NJ: Wiley.

Charney, R. S. (1998). *Teaching children to care: Management in the responsive classroom.* Greenfield, MA: Northeast Foundation for Children.

Coontz, S. (1992). *The way we never were: American families and the nostalgia trap.* New York, NY: Basic.

Faris, R., & Felmlee, D. (2014). Casualties of social combat: School networks of peer victimization and their consequences. *American Sociological Review, 79*, 228–257.

Flannery, K. B., Fenning, P., Kato, M. M., & McIntosh, K. (2014). Effects of school-wide positive behavioral interventions and supports and fidelity of implementation on problem behavior in high schools. *School Psychology Quarterly, 29*(2), 111.

Gutierrez, K. (2006). White innocence: A framework and methodology for rethinking educational discourse and inquiry. *International Journal of Learning, 12*(10). p. 223–229. 7p.

Hair, N. L., Hanson, J. L., Wolfe, B. L., & Pollak, S. D. (2015). Association of child poverty, brain development, and academic achievement. *JAMA Pediatrics, 169*(9), 822–829.

Harry, B., & Klingner, J. (2014). *Why are so many minority students in special education?* New York, NY: Teachers College Press.

Hollins, E. (1996). Culture in school learning: Revealing the deep meaning. Hillsdale, NJ: Lawrence Erlbaum.

Kamii, C. (1989). *Young children continue to reinvent arithmetic.* New York, NY: Teachers College Press.

Kavale, K. (1990). 'Differential programming in serving handicapped students'. In: Wang, M. C., Reynolds, M. and Wahlberg, H. J. (Eds) Special Education: Research and Practice. Oxford: Pergamon Press, pp. 35–55.

Knestrict, T (2017). The Special Education Industrial Complex. *Journal of Behavioral and Social Science. 3 (4).*

Kohn, A. (1999). *Punished by rewards: The trouble with gold stars, incentive plans, A's, praise, and other bribes.* New York: Houghton Mifflin Harcourt.

McLaren, P. (2015). *Life in schools: An introduction to critical pedagogy in the foundations of education* (6th ed.). New York, NY: Longman.

Oakes, J., Lipton, M., Anderson, L., & Stillman, J. (2015). *Teaching to change the world.* Boston: Routledge.

Piaget, J. (1965). *The moral judgement of the child.* New York, NY: Free Press. (Originally published 1932).

Picciano, A., & Spring, J. (2013). *The great American educational industrial complex.* New York, NY: Taylor Francis.

Pickett, K. E., & Wilkinson, R. G. (2015). Income inequality and health: A causal review. *Social Science & Medicine, 128,* 316–326.

Pink, D. H. (2011). *Drive: The surprising truth about what motivates us.* New York: Penguin.

Reschly, D. J. (1997). Assessment and eligibility determination in the Individuals with Disabilities Education Act of 1997. Washington D.C.: In *IDEA Amendments of 1997* (pp. 65–104).

Sloan-Cannella, G. (1997). *Deconstructing early childhood education: Social justice and revolution.* New York, NY: Peter Lang.

Wiliam, D. (2011). *Embedded formative assessment.* Bloomington, IN: Solution Tree Press.

· 5 ·

CHANGE NOT CONTROL

Reconstructing a Socially Just PBIS Model

Social Injustice Rectified Chapter Five:

1. *The new model encourages the development of autonomy.*
2. *The new model will deemphasize the concept of pathology.*
3. *The new model encourages and celebrates diversity.*
4. *The new model seeks to support the development of self-control and autonomy.*
5. *The new model will defend against construction of a hierarchy based on disability.*

The purpose of this final chapter is to describe the philosophical framework for the development of a more socially just and responsive PBIS model. In the previous chapters we have deconstructed the existing model and exposed several specific themes that are both ineffective and serve to control behavior rather than develop autonomy. This existing model was shown to emphasize control and served to maintain power structures that support the continued use of the model and also shown to hasten the identification of students with disabilities. The current model is algorithmic in form and values the final product of obedience and conformity rather than a more heuristic model that will emphasize the process of internalizing behavior change. Finally, the current

PBIS model has been shown to negatively affect the achievement of and to increase identification of children from underrepresented groups and students who are lower on the socioeconomic ladder (Harry & Klingner, 2014). This hierarchal framework is the direct product of the obedience-driven and pathology-creating model.

A new vision of PBIS was presented previously in Knestrict (2015). This chapter further develops the philosophical foundations of the new model while presenting a theoretical framework and practical applications of the new model and its use in schools. The newly reconstructed model will address the themes we uncovered in Chapters one to four. Through the uncovering of these deficiencies a series of broad, foundational themes are reconstructed to produce a foundation that will guide a more socially just and effective PBIS model. I will use the existing three-tiered model as a basic framework. However, the purpose and function of these tiers will be different.

Theme #1—Inside-Out Change—A Microsystem-Infused Ecological Change Model

Covey (1987) writes about the ineffectiveness of strategies that attempt to motivate people through personality or manipulate others into behaving in a way that someone else wants them to behave.

> It is the human endowment of independent will that makes effective self-management possible. It is the ability to act rather than be acted upon, to proactively carry out our (self-determined program). (p. 148)

Many developmental theorists including Piaget (1965) and have established that there are sequential stages of growth and development. That change happens in somewhat predictable, developmental steps or stages. We seem to have no problem accepting this fact when it applies to physical or cognitive growth. However, when it comes to affective growth and the development of an internal locus of control we do not consider this in the same way. Changing locus of control requires self-awareness, self-reflection, and a level of affective awareness that does not occur unless it is intentionally targeted and valued. It also requires environments that are caring and focused on building trusting relationships. Instead, we are inclined to rely on externally driven models that emphasize an immediate product of obedience or compliance rather than the long-term, process-oriented work of change. Covey (1987) uses a story of dealing with his child's behavior at a party to illustrate the difference between the two perspectives:

> I remember violating this principle myself as a father many years ago. One day I returned home to my little girls third-year birthday party to find her in the corner in the front room, defiantly clutching all of her presents, unwilling to let the other children play with them. The first thing I noticed was several parents in the room witnessing this selfish display. I was embarrassed, and doubly so because I was teaching a class in human relations and I knew, or at least felt, the expectations of these parents. (p. 38)

Because of his embarrassment Covey simply took control of the child's behavior, grabbed the presents from her, and distributed them to the other children to play with to the displeasure of his daughter. He pulled rank and punished his daughter. His thinking was that he would gain the immediate product of sharing the gifts whether it came from his daughter or not. He goes on to describe how the opinions of the parents and the perceived demands their opinions put upon the situation motivated him to take control and responsibility for his daughter's behavior. This occurs daily in schools. The expectations are driven not by the need to teach and model internal ways of managing behavior but from the outside expectations developed by those in power to ensure obedience and control. Covey (1987):

> Borrowing strength builds weakness. It builds weakness in the borrower because it reinforces dependence on external factors to get things done. It builds weakness in the person forced to acquiesce, stunting the development of independent reasoning, growth and internal discipline. It also builds weakness in the relationship. Fear replaces cooperation and both people involved become more arbitrary and defensive. (p. 39)

All internal change occurs from inside the individual and moves outward. This is counter to the way we intervene on behaviors of other people. A process perspective would look at learning these internal controls as developmental in nature, requiring the individual (i.e., Covey's daughter) to learn the value of sharing, the connectedness of her behavior to others, and the value in managing these moments personally as opposed to another person taking control. Clearly, this is a labor-intensive and a process-driven model that requires time, patience, and the luxury of making mistakes as well as the available guidance offered by more competent peers and adults. This more heuristic way of learning internal controls runs counter to the typical context of a school, which often uses a more direct instruction model of teaching new behaviors.

If the basic perspective changes and an internal locus of control model is utilized it is then that the existing ecosystems that envelope the child will also begin to change. In fact, if all children were taught within this context dramatic ecological change would occur. There are examples of this type of thinking that exist within schools today. However, they are often seen as marginal and not as rigorous. The Montessori method offers a clear process-driven model concerned with developing these inner controls using a more heuristic method that emphasizes process over product (Lillard, 2007). Also, the Responsive Classroom Technique (Rimm-Kaufman, Fan, Chiu, & You, 2007) describes this type of approach as an academic enabler as well as being more likely to assist in the development of an internal locus of control (Charney, 1998). However, within a standards-based reality spending time on these efforts is seen as soft and a waste of good academic time.

Within a new PBIS model this type of "inside-out thinking" fits within all three tiers and would be effective at the building-wide level or the smaller group or targeted levels. It would only require a change of thinking from strategies and systems that encourage a more product-oriented approach to a more proactive and interpersonal approach that creates relationships and community that surround the child and provide the examples and the contextual opportunity to learn, fail, and improve their ability to use an internal locus of control. Likewise, it is a global emphasis of doing things "with" children to develop these inner controls as opposed to doing things "to" children to control their behavior. It is a simple but fundamental difference and paradigm shift.

Theme #2—Responsiveness

These qualities in teachers are also linked with classrooms with a lower number of behavioral problems as well as more engagement in learning (Bear, 2015). There are five characteristics that Bear (2015) identifies:

(1) **Authenticity**—Being who you are and revealing your humanness to your students. When you are sad, tell them why. When you are angry, tell them why. When they witness this authenticity they will be more authentic. Many times children do not have an example of an adult who is truly authentic and trustworthy. Be that person.

(2) **Keeping Your Words and Actions Congruent**—If there is a classroom rule that states no eating of food in the classroom, follow it. If you bring in your donut and coffee and the kids see this, you lose credibility.

Walk the walk. Palmer (2007) also identifies this characteristic as crucial in building a trusting and caring classroom environment.

(3) **Full Disclosure**—This occurs when a teacher makes clear all criteria, expectations, and assumptions that guide practice and assignments in the class. In relation to behavior in the classroom many students will ask if there is a reason behind a specific rule. If so, provide it. Using the old adage of "Because I said so" is not credible and builds a wall between teacher and student. The development of classroom rules is a great place to start this ethos. Allow students to develop these rules and brainstorm the reasons why they would be a good rule or not. This discussion by itself will lend credibility to your classroom simply because you included them in the development of the rules.

(4) **Demonstrating Responsiveness**—Responsiveness is the act of demonstrating clearly that you want to know any concerns and problems students are having with their learning or any facet of the classroom, so you can help them deal with their concerns (Brookfield, 2015). This is another characteristic that they may not see examples of anywhere else but at school. The simple act of responding in a caring and concerned way to the needs of students provides a powerful counterbalance to what some students might be experiencing day to day. It builds trust.

(5) **Disclosing Personhood**—Show them that you are fully human, as opposed to teacher with a capital T. Tell them your story, your likes and dislikes. Share your family with them. Tell them how your weekend was and what you do with your free time. Providing an example of a fully human teacher can be a powerful moment in a child's life and it is linked to the development of children who are more caring as well (Kohn, 1995).

Daily Conversations

The Responsive Classroom (Charney, 1998) describes a technique they call the morning meeting. It is a classroom meeting involving all students at the beginning of the day. The rules, rituals, and routines that the morning meeting is a part of constitute the foundation of this approach to proactively intervene on student behavior. The function of the morning meeting is twofold. The first reason is to provide a morning ritual that greets the students and reminds them that they are involved in a group project of sorts. A project that they are a crucial element of. With the other students and adults, they are valued and respected and listened to. The second function is to provide a conduit for the teacher to communicate and practice the skills necessary for students to learn to be intrinsically motivated people. Being a valued member of something larger than themselves is a privilege, and students typically want to remain in such a group. To do so they must learn to monitor their own behavior. If they are unable to do so they will find themselves outside of this coveted group. This is not enforced by anyone. It is just a logical consequence of being human. If you are unable to live by the rules established by the group, then you cannot be a part of that group. The power of this is not in the hands of the teacher but collectively in the hands of the students. All of this is predicated on creating a classroom culture that students want to remain in. A question worth asking is, "are most classrooms designed to be this way; If not, why not?" PBIS systems are predicated on the assumption that the student needs to be offered a bribe to remain part of the group. Why is it necessary to bribe students? The teacher is called upon to engage the students in learning. It is well established that engaged students require no bribe to perform (Toldson, McGee, & Lemmons, 2017).

The new vision of Positive Behavioral Intervention Supports must be fundamentally founded upon this idea of responsiveness. In a culture as diverse as the United States, public schools are standardizing curriculum and behavioral strategies to a "one-size-fits-all" approach. It is ridiculous to assume that all students in all contexts will learn and achieve and, indeed, behave in the same way at the same level. Quality education, by its nature, is responsive and nonstandardized. Einstein's famous quote, "Everybody is a genius. But if you judge a fish by its ability to climb a tree, it will live its whole life believing that it is stupid," is particularly poignant in this discussion. It is the teacher's responsibility to find the way children learn best, be it academics or new behaviors. Responsiveness is at the heart of this responsibility. It is essential that a new vision of PBIS be premised upon this fundamental point. There are several existing examples of models that manifest this emphasis on responsiveness. Montessori provides four guiding principles that speak to responsiveness (Gutek, 1988). They are:

(1) **Each child is to be respected**—Children, even children with severe behavioral difficulties, deserve our respect. They are children who are still forming, and like a child who needs support in learning to read, some children need support in learning new ways of behaving, communicating, and existing in a community. Especially when working with students with difficult behaviors it becomes challenging to

maintain respect for the student. One teacher in a school I observed in preparation for this book, stated the following:

> Even the most miserably behaving child deserves, at least, my acceptance of him as a human being. He is still growing and learning and while he may be trying to push me away with his behaviors it may be, ironically, that is how he thinks he can get my attention and love. (teacher comments at IAT)

Years of research reinforce the notion that it is in fact these children who need connection. These children require respect and an environment that will teach them how to gain control over themselves.

(2) **All children can learn**—they can't always do so at the same rate as someone else, or at the same level but all children can learn. This becomes very important when we are teaching children alternative ways of existing within a community.

(3) **The first six years of a child's life is a sensitive period for all learning**—because children are predisposed to learning at this age and because the excitement of learning has not been killed, yet the ages between 0 and 6 are particularly fertile. During these ages a child absorbs what it sees. Children may not be able to implement these things yet but they see them (Montessori, 1949). If they are presented with an ordered and predictable environment with adults and older, more competent children existing together in an orderly and predictable way, they form schemas of these structures in their minds. Later in this age period when they are able to implement these behaviors autonomously they already have the existing schema available to them and they can access it immediately. Alternatively, if they do not have these schemas, and have not been provided these examples, they struggle and often fall back on the examples they have seen and their behavior becomes disruptive to the community.

(4) **Children naturally enjoy learning and working hard if allowed to direct their learning**—the natural state of young children is curiosity and engagement in their learning (Montessori, 1949). This includes all children. The separation of children on account of ability or disability is seen by this new vision of PBIS as counterproductive. The secret really becomes finding what engages the learner and then providing that for them. It is only after we strip them of their control over their environment and curriculum that they become less engaged. Fundamentally children need to be involved in deciding what they

learn, how they learn it, and developing the rules of the community they exist in. It is the focus on sequenced and paced curriculum and testing that often leads to disengagement in students.

It is the aim of this new model that children with these behavioral issues need more connection and more affective responsiveness to become an autonomous adult. So much so that these behavioral efforts should take precedence over academics entirely. For example, in our current education and PBIS models there is an assumption that school can both address the behavioral and affective needs of students while at the same time moving them forward academically. Fundamental to a new way of understanding PBIS is coming to the realization that this is a myth. Targeting growth in locus of control and self-discipline trumps all else and if it does not, then real change will not occur. In addition, real academic growth will stop as well.

Theme #2—The Cosmic Classroom and the Human Potential

Whole to Part Learning

Fundamental to a new PBIS perspective is the pedagogical strategy of Whole to Part Learning. This tenet is usually ascribed to academic learning, but it is equally valid when teaching social skills and appropriate behavior within a community. Currently we focus on teaching discrete pieces of information moving toward a larger understanding (Sunal & Haas, 2002). For example, in social studies methods, we teach pre-service teachers to teach from the student outward. Teach them about home and family, then neighborhood and community outward to the world, solar system and universe (Seefeldt, Castle, & Falconer, 2014). However, this does not allow the student to perceive the larger whole and their place within this larger whole, until the end of the unit of learning. Montessori (1948/1973) describes the importance of starting with the whole and presenting the universe first and showing the student that even amidst this infinite universe we are there, a part of this highly organized and unbelievably large universe. The Montessori method has stories that they tell of the creation of the universe. These stories serve to provide an order to the learning and a cosmic connection to each individual. It is the connection of the larger concepts to the child as an individual that provides for them a schema or framework of understanding for all of the details between the universe, solar system, Earth, community, neighborhood, and home. This concept is illustrated by stacking blocks on the floor in a tower. The largest serves as the base, and subsequent smaller boxes are used to create the tower. On top is a small human being. The universe is like this. It is systematically organized from large to small and we human beings are connected to this universe even though we are very small in comparison.

This context is crucial to directing the learning of the child. This context is often what is missing when we are teaching children about making choices with our behavior within a community. If we teach that we are all part of the larger community, existing together in this classroom as a unit, we create a community that requires rules to guide our choices so that everyone can thrive. We allow students to be part of the rule-making and the culture-building of their classroom. It is then we have reason for making good choices as a community member. We create a schema that communicates the privilege of being in this group. If we match this with engaging learning activities, we have a community that children will want to be a part of and will choose behaviors that allow them to stay.

Imagination and Learning

Montessori (1948/1973) details the importance of accessing the child's imagination as part of the learning process. She gives examples of young children needing to begin to understand that "life is a cosmic agent," presenting a big picture of the universe and the Earth as not discrete facts but as living concepts with direct connections to the student. The same can be true with the learning ways of being within a community or a classroom. Discussing and imagining how your behavior makes another feel, how your actions might affect another, or how your wants may impact the wants and needs of others, these discussions are processed with children through imagination first and then, after the schema have been formed, they play out in real time in the classroom. With this new way of intervening on behaviors it is more about what we do with children, how we prepare the environment and experiences they will live through than it is about what we do to children to get them to act the way we want them to.

This lack of spiritual connection is a deep flaw within current PBIS and education in general. This is not a religious structure or framework. But it is a cosmic or spiritual one. Teaching children they are connected to everything in the world, the Earth, the ground, the school and each other is a perspective that is lacking in our almost paranoid effort in preventing anything spiritual inside a public school. But it is this type of foundational community building that differentiates environments focusing on the development of an internal locus of control (Rimm-Kaufman & Hulleman, 2007.

Theme # 3—Autonomy Is the Goal of Education

Piaget (1965), Kamii (1989), Kamii and Clark (1993), and Montessori (1974) write at length about the importance of developing several types of autonomy including emotional, intellectual, and physical. Through this development of autonomy also grows an internal locus of control that is at the heart of this new vision for PBIS (Steiner, 2016). To develop any type of autonomy the child must be given control over their environment and then guided in their choices. The current PBIS goes to great lengths to "bribe" students to behave in the way that those in power require. Obedience-driven models require someone to make the demands upon the students. If we structure a school and a PBIS model so that the students develop the norms, police the norms, and individually choose to live by those norms we teach them autonomy. Choice and control of their learning is at the center of the development of autonomy and the development of an internal locus of control (Montessori,1949). If you look at how schools organize themselves it is an obedience model even for the teachers in the building. The principal is given a set of operating standards handed to him/her from the district and state and teachers implement. The principal also has a particular viewpoint on how the school should be run and the teachers' implement. The teachers, given the expectations of the author-ity above them, run the classroom in a way that will fulfill those expectations. It is all a "top-down" organization founded upon values that are established outside of the individual and implemented in a way as to please the authority in charge.

Students Forming the Rules

How would it look different if the stakeholders in the schools and classrooms developed the norms? In an obedience-driven PBIS model the school rules and classroom rules are typically provided for the students. They represent what the monolithic culture values, which is obedience and order in the drive to improve test scores. Obedience is valued because it allows those in power to quickly and effectively create the order necessary for instruction and higher test scores and the perceived increased value of the school and its curriculum. Tier one methods reflect the values that create the necessary environment for order. Appropriate rewards for obedience are created. There is often an effort to allow students to create these rewards. In fact, in ABA practice this is recommended (Alberto & Troutman, 2012).

A tier one model I observed in preparation for this book used a system that required teachers to catch students being good. When the staff observed appropriate behavior they filled out a slip of paper with the child's name on it. It was placed in a basket and used for a drawing for prizes. The more times you got your name placed in the basket the higher your chance of winning. Rather than encouraging obedience it seemed to create a self-serving shrewdness and competitive vibe encouraging students to elicit attention from staff members. In addition, it was the same 25 students receiving the preponderance of the attention and slips filled out. Be careful what you create. Reward systems such as this look very attractive to students initially. However, remember the Hedonic Adaptation effect. As the year progressed the rewards grew less motivational for students and the staff inflated the rewards to maintain the interest of the students.

Punishment or what is deceptively called "negative or natural consequences" are also developed. Thus, those in power create everything and enforce everything. From a student's perspective this system is imposed on them.

In contrast, an autonomy-driven tier one model would begin and end with the students. The Northeast Foundation in the Responsive Classroom Technique has already developed a vivid example of how this would look. It begins on the first day of school. It must be stated that the Responsive Classroom Technique emphasizes that the entire first six weeks of school are to be focused not on new academic learning but on establishing building the caring community of the classroom. The following description is derived from Charney (1998). In September the students are led through a discussion that asks them to identify their "hopes and dreams" for the coming year. Students will list all sorts of ideas like "multiplication" or "reading" to "having fun" "going on field trips," In one classroom I observed in preparation for this book a second grade student, aware that the school had purchased a 3D printer, stated that it was his hope and dream to make lots of stuff on the 3D printer! Once these hopes and dreams are recorded the teacher talks to the students about how the classroom should function so that all of our hopes and dreams will come true. The students see this for the cue on developing rules that it is and begin to share their thoughts. The teacher needs to be skilled at facilitating this process and moving it toward the development of broad, values-based rules for the classroom. Some classrooms call the rules "procedures" or "agreements." The suggested number of rules is typically between 3 and 5. They should be stated positively. For example, a rule might say, "Be kind to each other" as opposed to "Don't be mean." There is no time spent on the development of rewards or consequences. The rules are only tied to their hopes and dreams and the functioning of the classroom. They are broad and values based because in a classroom emphasizing a process of learning new ways of choosing your behavior the emphasis is not catching them being bad or good but discussing with them when they make good or bad choices. At that moment, in that context, discuss more appropriate ways of behaving that align with the classroom rules and culture. Give reason for the desired behavior and pointing out why we feel that it's important to behave in that way. All of these discussions are linked backed to hopes and dreams and the community rules of operation. If it is an engaging classroom that is fun to learn in and if all of the individuals like and care about each other then they will want to remain a valued member making aligned choices easier. This approach takes a lot of time and effort. It will take time away from academic instruction. The idea is that these "lessons learned" early will benefit the learning environment later.

Theme #4—Preparing the Environment

Rules, Rituals, and Routines

The preparation of the classroom environment includes creating the rules, rituals, and routines that are needed for a community to function. Knestrict (2006) defines rules as three to five broadly based, values based goals for behavior within the community. Rituals are defined as routines that take on a greater meaning and bring people together in the community. An example of a ritual in the home would be the bedtime routine. Structuring this routine is necessary for the tasks of cleaning, dressing, and preparing for bed. However, because of the closeness of these bedtime routines, they often evolve into rituals. Cuddling, saying a prayer, or reading a bedtime story allows the parent and child to become closer both physically and emotionally. Consistent routines and rituals also provide a child with a schema of predictability that allows them to organize their emotional thoughts and feelings around. Routines are defined as doing the same thing in the same way at the same time everyday (Knestrict, 2006). The predictability of a community that is based upon consistent rules, rituals, and routines allows children to form schema that tells them that life is predictable, consistent, and supportive of the community and each individual. The more routinized a classroom environment is the fewer office referrals there are (Knestrict, 2006).

Preparing the Individual

Preparing the environment also includes the preparation of the teacher for teaching (Montessori, 1965). Lesson plans, schedules, and knowing the flow of the day are necessary in maintaining the predictability that is crucial as a proactive management strategy. More importantly is the preparation for teaching within this new model of PBIS. James Comer states, "there is no significant learning without significant relationships" (Payne, 1996, p. 9). Responsiveness is the characteristic of being an authentic and concerned human being first (Charney, 1998). This is an essential characteristic of effective teaching in a more responsive PBIS model. In addition to responsiveness is the willingness to divulge your own "personhood" (Brookfield, 2015). This harkens back to the idea of the cosmic classroom and illustrates for students a connectedness to each other that many teachers within the current PBIS model find uncomfortable. Connecting with students and responding to their emotional as well as their intellectual needs is crucial when providing a model for humanness and an example of how to function within a community. Kohn (1995) shares a story about meeting his first grade teacher at the grocery store when he was young. He noticed that she was buying cereal and food just like his mom! Somehow this event exposed the humanness of the teacher and she became a human being as opposed to a TEACHER. She was more relatable and more accessible. This type of humanizing moment is essential in a responsive PBIS model and important in a model that doesn't play on power relationships.

Spiritual Preparation

Montessori (1974) wrote prophetically about the importance of teachers becoming what she called "spiritually" prepared for teaching. This was referring to more of a constant state of reflection as opposed to an actually spiritual experience. However, the emotional and spiritual growth that occurs as a result of this level of reflection can often feel like a spiritual awakening. She writes:

> We insist on the fact that a teacher must prepare herself interiorly by systematically studying herself so that she can tear out her most deeply rooted defects, those in fact that which impede her relationships with children … we must begin to see ourselves as others see us. (p. 149)

This process can take place in pre-service and must continue throughout the teacher's career. As the teacher begins to interact with children and as the community is formed it again becomes important for the teacher to provide an example of self-reflection, and sharing this with children can illustrate this for them. This is not to suggest that you share deeply personal reflections but to more model the meta-cognitive ability to reflect by telling the children "boys and girls I was thinking about how I spoke to you all yesterday when I was angry and I want to apologize for raising my voice, I will try not to do that again when I am angry. Can you help me remember that?"

Joyous Observer

"Teachers must shed their omnipotence and become the joyous observer" (Montessori, 1948/2005, p. 103). Letting go of the "controller" persona of a classroom teacher and assuming a more facilitative observer role is very difficult for many teachers. This hegemonic tendency is an artifact of a product-oriented curriculum and is prevalent in standards-based classrooms. If the quality of your teaching were being judged by how well you move through the standards, then control would have to be used because children will often not move at the pace that you wish. Therefore, bribes are offered in the guise of behavioral intervention plans to motivate students to move to the next set of standards. When we force the pace and the content of the learning, children will rebel and external control will be needed. Better to allow students to choose areas of interest and, more importantly, the pace of their learning. This encourages autonomy and is also correlated with fewer office behavior referrals (Annamma, Morrison, & Jackson, 2014).

Theme # 5—Growth Mindset

With a growth mindset, students believe that their abilities can be developed through hard work. Raw talent and IQ are just starting points. A growth mindset perspective creates a love of learning and a resilience that is essential for deep learning. This way of being allows students to relax and know that over time they will learn what you are teaching them (Dweck & Rule, 2013). This is not tied to pacing of curriculum; it is not based upon standardized methods or tests. It is based on deep learning at the pace that the individual requires. A community that bases itself on a growth mindset can utilize the synergy of the group to propel all members further and deeper into their learning (Covey, 1987). As regards PBIS a growth mindset can benefit students whose behavior is initially counterproductive to the larger group. Because of the growth mindset the group and the individual can feel confident that the behaviors will change and the synergy that is created by a responsive and well-developed community will help support the individual in gaining control over their behavioral choices. The group is fundamental to the development of the individual.

Theme #6—Intervention Is "Outside In"

With a new vision of PBIS being founded upon a belief and practices focusing on the change agent being the child, it seems counterintuitive to speak of behavioral interventions being fundamentally looked at from an "outside in" perspective. When a child does not respond to the tier one strategies that will be founded upon these themes described earlier, tier two and three interventions might be warranted. The flow of these efforts will always progress from outside of the child toward the child.

In Japan if a child is failing, teachers take this as their failure. This is not to advocate teachers simply taking the blame for all things in the classroom. However, it does bring to mind a way of thinking that creates an order of operations when developing interventions. An order that looks at the exterior ecosystems first and works back toward the child. An ecologically based intervention model would begin to analyze behavioral issues starting first with the teacher, the exo- and meso-system variables, and would only move toward the child as needed. So the interveners would begin by looking at teaching, engagement, differentiation, rules, rituals and routines, Developmentally Appropriate Practice (DAP) home to school transitions, or other "outside the child" variables. Too often Intervention Assistance Teams (IAT) shoot directly for the child, or identify deficits and structure bribes to motivate the student to behave in the way they wish them to behave. Often interventions are used to hasten the identification of a child and this new vision for PBIS will discourage this practice.

Travis and the Tantrums

In preparation for this book a second grade classroom was observed. There was a seven-year-old boy named Travis (not his real name). He was brought before the IAT. Travis would become physically and verbally aggressive around 11:00 am and again at 2:00 pm. He would cause great disruption and the tier one ticket program described earlier was not working for Travis and a handful of other children. The tier two bribes on top of the ticket system controlled the behavior except for Travis. His behavior was only increasing in energy and frequency. The classroom teacher brought Travis before the IAT and described his behavior as violent, aggressive, out of control, making instruction for Travis and all of the other students impossible. The first effort of an intensive and targeted intervention plan consisted of additional bribes and threats of punishments as well as an additional ticket system that was targeting the aggressive outbursts. The teacher as well as members of the IAT also stated that an ETR might be called for and the sooner we could provide those supports the better for Travis and the others.

The future had already been determined for Travis and the current behavioral plan was a means to an end. However, the teacher who team-taught with the presenting teacher had other ideas. She looked into other environmental variables. In essence she started outside of Travis and began looking at variables in the environment first. She had a different experience with Travis and worked with him when he was engaged and learning. This teacher discovered that Travis had a 45-minute bus ride in the morning to get to school. He typically ate breakfast at 6:00 am, caught the bus at 6:30, arrived at school at 7:15 and did not eat lunch until 12:30. He would go to lunch but loved to play on the playground and often did not eat his lunch or ate only a small part of it, before he went out to play. This teacher had a son with diabetes and had witnessed how her son's behavior changed when his blood sugar was low and thought this might be the reason Travis was struggling. She simply fed a small snack to Travis at 10:30 a.m. and made sure he ate his lunch before going out on the playground and then provided another snack at 1:30. He didn't have diabetes but he was hungry! Travis never had issues again.

This illuminated the value in looking outside the child first and not looking at possible deficits within the child. The hunger triggered some of these behaviors and these were technically "within" Travis. It was the practice of looking for ecological variables, like the hour that he ate his first meal at home, that made the difference. Again and again in my observations I saw the

IAT rush to identify children. In all of the IAT meetings I attended the presenting teacher never began by looking at the outside variables. Junior high and high school IAT teams were even more resistant to this way of thinking. In fact, several of the high schools observed had no real IAT structure or intervention model beyond groups to facilitate identification and placement. In some ways the older the student the less likely teachers were willing to look at anything causing the behavior other than the disobedience of the child and the quicker they were likely to pursue special education identification or removal from the class.

The Change Continuum

With the six themes in mind a theoretical framework has been developed reflecting and emphasizing the themes derived from the deconstruction process. The continuum is the tool that will be used to create the new system and help create the operating procedures that will ensure a more effective and socially just intervention model. This model targets change of behavior and the development of an internal locus of control in all students. A representation of this model is seen in Figure 5.1.

Theoretically professionals using this new model would begin constructing their contextually driven process prior to any behaviors occurring in the classroom, possibly before children even enter the classroom. If we begin by preparing the environment and other meso- and exo-system variables, the proactive and preparatory tasks will serve to prevent problematic behaviors. The left side of the continuum (Proactive) consists of practices that educators can do "with" or "for" children to facilitate an inner locus of control, develop language that assists in learning intellectual and behavioral autonomy. This side also consists of the things that need to be addressed prior to behavior and prior to any management techniques imposed "onto" children. The right side of the continuum represents a philosophical decision by the teacher or the intervention team that control is seen as more important than the development of an inner locus of control. Currently, teachers and teams jump to these methods almost immediately, producing the outcomes we have described in previous chapters. It is the aim of this model to limit the use of the right side control techniques to incidents that cause a care and safety concern to students and faculty. For example, if a student becomes physically aggressive and is deemed a threat to themselves or others, it would be appropriate to intervene in a way that takes control and ensure the safety of everyone. Remember the research

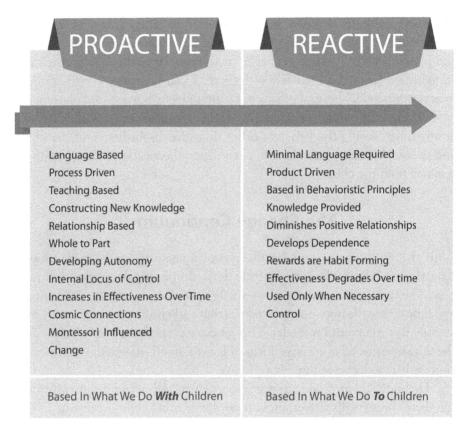

Figure 5.1 Ecological Model for Supports and Problem Solving. Source: Author.

that tells us that 3–5% of children require external control in school (Björn, Aro, Koponen, Fuchs, & Fuchs, 2015). Barring that, the development of an internal locus of control would take precedent over these methods and even academics if necessary. The line dividing the two sides is tilted to emphasize the left side of the continuum. The right side control-driven techniques are used judiciously and only when control is deemed more important than the development of an internal locus of control. Having said that, however, it doesn't mean that we abandon the left side techniques even if we require using control techniques. Rather, we continue using the left side even if, temporarily, we utilize control technologies on the right.

Left Side Characteristics

The left side of the continuum should be thought of in the same way that tier one interventions are thought of in the existing model. In other words, these are strategies that are school wide, used in every classroom, and ubiquitous. This side of the continuum will contain many of the things that are not currently thought of as management or intervention related but that will serve to "pay forward" and prevent acting out behaviors from occurring and will also provide the appropriate schema for students to learn to manage their own behaviors and impulses. The building of trusting, caring relationships between students and teachers and between students is at the heart of all of the strategies on the left side of the continuum. There are several other important characteristics of this side that need to be described. It is based in the idea that there are things we should do "with" children to teach them an internal locus of control and to be autonomous.

Preparing the Environment

- *Learning about students*—looking through and studying the cumulative files of each student, contacting and discussing about student with the previous year's teachers, discussing any interventions or behavioral concerns that were addressed. Also discussing the preferred way this child learns.
- *Getting to know students and families*—in the old days this used to mean sending a letter or postcard to the student in the summer to introduce yourself to the child and family. Now it is beneficial to meet the family and the child in person and make several contacts throughout the summer in preparation for the year. Establishing these relationships makes huge deposits in the child's and the family's trust bank accounts (Covey, 1987). There is a correlation between high levels of trust and cooperation with students and families (Covey, 1987).
- *Communication plan with students and families*—during the relationship building develop an agreed-upon method of communication between home and school. Make sure that this communication is reciprocal and that the parent realizes that you are available for contact at specific times during the day. This will limit unnecessary interruptions and foster communication.

- *Fellowship events at school*—as part of the tier one of the new model planned fellowship events should be developed by the leadership of the school. Sharing a meal with families is a great vehicle for developing these events. These events also are correlated with a higher level of trust and cooperation with families and students. Family engagement has also been shown to decrease school violence (Boulter, 2004), improve graduation rates, and increase the likelihood that early adolescents will enroll in higher education (Deslandes & Bertrand, 2005).
- *Covenant with families and student*—the new model advocates an agreement be signed between the student, the family, and the school that serves as a "covenant." A covenant is a promise that contains a spiritual piece to it. It suggests that the needs of the child will outweigh the needs of the teachers or the parents. Expanding the definition of engagement is the first step for schools in creating socially just environments for students and adults. Engagement is founded upon building relationships in which teachers and parents respect one another, believe in each other's ability and willingness to fulfill their responsibilities, have high personal regard for one another, and trust each other to put children's interests first (Bryk & Schneider, 2002; Henderson et al., 2006).
- *School Social Worker establishing connections with families and school (conduit)*—assigning one person responsible for daily and weekly communication between school and family. This would be in addition to daily or weekly contact from teachers. This separate position would allow someone besides the teacher to deal with attendance issues or issues of lack of parent involvement, maintaining the often fragile trusting relationship between teacher and parents. Some districts call these positions "visiting teachers," referring to the home visits that would be part of the job. I prefer school social worker because I feel it describes more accurately the purpose of the position.
- *Rules, Rituals, and Routine*—there are three crucial facets of preparing the classroom environment that serve as a proactive strategy in avoiding problematic student behaviors. These are often called the three "silver bullets" of prevention. They are rules, rituals, and routines.
  - *Rules*—are the three to five, values-based rules described in previous chapters. They are developed and designed by the students, with the assistance of the teacher. They serve as teaching tools to guide practice in the classroom and to allow students to achieve the "hopes and dreams" they identified as their goals at the beginning of

the school year. They serve as guides for behavior and for points of reference for teaching new behaviors with students.

o *Rituals*—rituals are defined as routines with meaning (Knestrict, 2006). The meaning of "ritual" in this context being that routines serve to draw people closer together. The fellowship nights could be an example of a ritual activity. These rituals add depth to a community and purpose to some of the routines communities have.

o *Routines*—routines are defined as organizing activities that are done in the same way, at the same time, everyday. In a school and a classroom there are activities—home room, attendance, daily schedule, restroom breaks—that structure the day, create a high level of predictability, and create a day that is consistent and predictable for teachers and students alike (Knestrict, 2006).

Preparing the Curriculum

Developmentally Appropriate Practice—When considering what students need to learn and how to best engage them in learning there are several known practices that can guide us. There is a positive correlation between deep engagement and fewer behavioral issues in the classroom (Gartrell, 2002). (Copple and Bredekamp (2009) Bredekamp & Kopple, 1997) list six guidelines for curriculum and pedagogy that maximizes achievement, engagement, and, in turn, will limit behavioral issues. They are:

1) Creating a caring community of learners where each member of the community is respected, has the opportunity to create and maintain supportive and caring relationships

2) Creating a community where children feel safe.

3) Creating a community where there is a clear, reasonable, and predictable environment developed, helping children reflect and understand the reasons for rules, rituals, and routines.

4) Using developmentally appropriate practices to enhance development and learning.

5) Authentically assessing children's development and learning using formative and criterion-referenced assessments.

6) Forming and maintaining reciprocal relationships with families.

Montessori practice informs our preparation of the curriculum by adding the importance of using multiple data points to accurately assess learning of individual students. There is also an emphasis of increasing time on task and developing what Csikszentmihalyi (1997) called "flow," which is a deep state of learning and learning satisfaction. This is also positively correlated to an internal locus of control (Csikszentmihalyi, 1997). Finally, because of the emphasis of "whole to part" learning, the new model advocates the development of relationships with the greater community that the school exists in.

Language and Constructivist Based—There is an intentional focus on language with all strategies on the left side of the continuum. This is because we know that to become meta-cognitive language is the vital ingredient in learning anything new, including new ways of being (Vygotsky, 1978). With all new schemas that are developed there is a vocabulary developing as well. In fact, it is well documented that the lack of language capability is often a precursor to acting out behaviors (Rao & Landa, 2014). As a result, all of the strategies on this side of the continuum have an intentional language piece involved. It should also be noted that since these strategies are considered universal or tier one a common language for staff and students is extremely valuable and useful in teaching new ways of being within a group. For example, many schools use a common language to encourage children to understand that behavior is a choice. Using the phrase "stop and think" proves useful in cuing children to systematically think about choices and outcomes for those choices. This common language will decrease impulsive behavior choices.

Language is central to reflection and the interaction that is necessary in a more responsive intervention model. For example, Gartrell (2002) talks about using a "guidance approach." This entails discussions about various choices of behavior. Rather than simply administering a consequence upon witnessing the behavior the teacher in a more responsive intervention model would discuss the choices the child made, the outcomes of the choice, and possible other "better" choices as well. This language-driven process, over time, allows the student to construct an understanding of the role that context has in behavior choice. It also aids in the development of a schema or framework of understanding that can be used again in a similar situation (Kamii, 1989; Piaget, 1965). It is this language-based construction of schema that allows children to develop an internal locus of control. It is the development of prior learning experiences that serves as the foundation of later internalization. Constructivism states that learning is an active, constructive process. The learner is an information constructor. People actively construct or create their own representations of reality. New information is linked to prior knowledge, thus mental representations are subjective (Trawick-Smith, 2017). In the context of behavioral change many children have no prior knowledge of what appropriate self-management is, so that initial experience has to be felt and reflected upon before new behaviors are taken on. If we establish a safe, nurturing, and supportive environment filled with people whom you care about and who care about you, you can safely and effectively experience those initial learning moments and build upon them.

Process Driven—Strategies on the left are process driven. In practice this means that the learning of an internal locus of control is something that will require many moments of practice, counseling, discussion, reflection, and interaction within the group to master. So the quick fix goal of an ABA approach will not be satisfied using these strategies. However, real behavioral change will occur over time. Like learning to run a marathon, it takes day after day after day of training to reach the point of being able to run. The same is true with learning to manage your own behavior. The teacher should also prepare himself or herself for this reality. Facilitating and coaching new ways of being is time consuming and labor intensive. But there is a payoff. If the teacher takes the first six weeks of school to teach the rules, rituals, and routines that were established by the class and build a trust with students that you are aware of the tediousness of the learning process behavior improves (Wong & Wong, 2004).

Teaching Based—The emphasis on the left side is always on teaching. However, the teaching of new behaviors and new ways of being cannot be limited by teaching these skills in a discrete course or class. These skills are embedded in the culture of the room. Working on new behaviors can occur when the class is walking down the hallway to lunch or in a private moment between a teacher and student. It can also happen between two students or a student and a teacher from another classroom. It needs to be implemented within the context of the school day. There are no worksheets or standards or curriculum. It requires language, discussion, and time.

Relationships—The building and living within significant relationships is at the heart of this new approach to management and intervention. There is no significant learning without significant relationships (Comer, 2010). Throughout the entire continuum, even if we are still externally controlling student behavior and using the right side of this continuum the relationship between teacher and student is the most important variable in the classroom. It is the essential first step in this new model and no further movement will matter much until this is attained. It should also be mentioned that this pertains to teacher–parent relationships as well. Nothing will matter much in the classroom unless you have full "buy in" and support from the parents of your children. They need to feel that you care about them and their child. In the Responsive Classroom approach it is typically a foundational principle that students need to "know" others and "be known" by others (Rimm-Kaufman et al., 2007).

Change/Internal Locus/Autonomy—The end goal we have in mind for all students is for them to develop an internal locus of control, develop intellectual as well as emotional and behavioral autonomy, and to learn to change their own behavior. The research is pretty clear that these types of significant change cannot happen with only rewards and punishments. It requires a systemic, global, process, over time within the context of meaningful relationships and a supportive and nurturing environment.

These strategies increase with effectiveness over time. As the student gains more control over their choices they begin to self-monitor and they become meta-cognitive. They form schema for appropriate behavior for existing in a group and they can monitor and reflect upon their own choices.

Cosmic Connections—The most beautiful and elegant part of the new model is the Cosmic Connection, teaching the idea that all human beings make choices with their behavior and all of us require the support of the community to learn how to make those good choices and to be aware of how our choices can affect the larger group and that we are all connected in a very real and tangible way. This ethic of community and connectedness is fostered rather than a competitive environment. The pie is bigger and there is enough for everyone (Covey, 1987). This strategy and way of thinking also implies that we all can learn to do these things by ourselves without external control. Not only can all of us do this but we will be better for it and happier as well.

Right Side Characteristics

What Necessitates a Shift to the Right Side?

It is assumed that the left side of the model is considered the universal tier one for all interventions. Likewise, it is assumed that all tier two and three interventions developed will reflect a majority of "left side" related ideas as well. All interventions, both targeted and individualized, will first reflect a majority of "left side" strategies. A move to the right side of the continuum is only necessitated by a determination by the team (which can and should include the student and the parent when appropriate) that control is more important than developing an internal locus of control. It is temporary and should only be considered when the behaviors manifested by the student are deemed as a threat to self or others. It is hypothesized that this would apply to less than 3–5% of the student population if all other "left side" strategies were utilized effectively (Berrios & Jacobowitz, 1998; Persi & Pasquali, 1999). It is also advised that even if the student is seen as a threat to self or others again the IAT should proceed systematically and begin interventions by looking at the environmental variables first before jumping to more behavioral methods or even physical restraint. It has been suggested that the rate of physical or even medicated restraints is higher for African-Americans than for other racial groups (Segal, Bola, & Watson, 1996). A systematic and disciplined approach of documentation, leveled interventions, and a more responsive PBIS is hypothesized to reduce the need for reactive interventions including physical restraints.

Deon and Assaultive Behavior

In preparation for the writing of this book I observed an IAT meeting in an urban elementary school. This episode illustrates why a shift to the right side of the continuum is sometimes necessary. It also shows that maintaining the "Outside in" problem-solving model is still important to use and that the left side of the continuum and the relationship-based interventions still play an important part even if tier three/right side interventions are being utilized. The student the group was problem-solving for was named Deon (not real name). Deon had not shown growth over time with the implementation of tier one and tier two interventions. These interventions had grown increasingly punitive and increasingly restrictive and controlling. The student had demonstrated a tendency to escalate and become physically assaultive, and there was one documented incident of another student being injured as a result of Deon's behavior. The realities of this student's behavior required a shift to the right side of the continuum. It was considered more important because of the safety of Deon and others to value control of the assaultive behavior over the concentration of developing an inner locus of control. Notice though that we only move to the right side, as it relates to the assaultive behavior, not all behaviors. This is an important distinction. IATs have a tendency to move the entire tier three intervention to the right and only emphasize control over the student and cease teaching Deon strategies to manage his own behavior in lieu of control strategies. They often use care and safety as the justification for doing so. However, while Deon did display assaultive behavior it still was in targeted situations under specific circumstances. The intervention, therefore, reflected this and was still heavily weighted toward the left side intervention strategies. The assaultive behavior piece of the plan prescribed restraints that would be implemented to ensure the care and safety of Deon and the other students when he became assaultive.

The majority of the tier three intervention plan was still attempting to teach Deon ways of controlling his anger and controlling himself. It was noticed that Deon's assaultive behaviors occurred at a specific time during the day and on days when he was staying with his mom and had an extra long bus ride to school. It turns out that Deon also did not get much sleep during his time with his mom and came to school very tired. This made him more likely to act out. In fact, all of the assaultive incidents occurred during these times with mom. We brought mom into the process and discussed what we had learned. Deon's mom worked two jobs. She did not return home from work until later in the evening and Deon was with an aunt until her return. Mom discussed the situation with the aunt, structured a schedule for Deon and his aunt, and his sleep increased. His assaultive behaviors decreased. This intervention was a direct result of the "outside in" problem-solving model and the IAT's fidelity in "outside in" problem solving, even with the most extreme behaviors.

The current PBIS model typically moves from less restrictive interventions to more restrictive interventions, indicating an increased emphasis on control of the individual and more rewards and punishments. There is an increase in punitive responses in tier three as well. In a more responsive model we would emphasize the targeting of behaviors while still deeply valuing the teaching of self-control. There is also a tendency of IAT to see tier three interventions as not another opportunity for the student to succeed but as the final, probably not going to be successful effort, before we recommend the student for special education evaluation. This trend is very dangerous and leads to the slippery slope of identification of students with a specific disability.

Difference Finding in the Current Model

Currently the PBIS model, FBA, and ABA are all based upon finding the differences in children and attempting to modify student behavior back to "normal." I observed a third grade student in a social studies class recently. He was a very intelligent child but lacked some social confidence and tended to want to work alone as a result. The teacher mandated a group project and assigned this young man to a group with two other boys. This created anxiety for this child and his behavior seemed to escalate. He felt this and went over to the reading center to sit in the beanbag chair to relax. When the teacher noticed, the student told the teacher that he was relaxing because he didn't like to work in groups. The teacher told him that he needed to get over to the group and help them or lose points for not working. His behavior escalated further, became disruptive, and he was removed from the class. If the teacher would have seen the coping strategy the student was using rather than the "difference" in the observable behavior might this event have been avoided? How many "events" occur because of this obsession with observable behavior and lack of tolerance of "other ways of thinking?"

Culture is often at the root of behavior escalations too. In a previous study Knestrict and Schoensteadt (2005) found that lack of cultural understanding often encouraged behavioral problems in students. Code shifting is the ability to shift the language code to fit the contextual needs of a situation (Gee, 1998; Joos, 1967; Montano-Harmon, 1991). When information is being taught in the classroom using a formal code of the English language, students in poverty often do not understand what is being said because of their lack of awareness in using the formal code (Payne, 1996). If behavioral directions are being communicated via a formal code of the English language and the students do not respond because of their lack of understanding it is often seen as an issue of insubordination when it is really an issue of translation (Knestrict & Schoensteadt, 2005). Observable behavior would miss this subtle precursor to behavior. Often all that is observed is the inappropriate behavior that was a result of miscommunication.

There is a hunt for difference in the current PBIS model and in education as a whole (Baglieri & Knopf, 2004). Historically Foucault (2007) spoke of this when he described the impact of medicine and medical thinking on the power relationships it creates. This can also be said of the pseudo-scientific medical-ization of difference in schools. Behavioral difficulties if intervened upon at all are often quickly shifted to a context of special education and a labeling of the student with Severe Emotional Disturbance. This pseudo-psychological definition and label gives a medical legitimacy to special education that is not warranted (Knestrict, 2017; Thomas & Loxley, 2001). The definition of the disability grouping of Emotional Disturbance is problematic and serves as a convenient dumping ground for students with behaviors that prove challeng-ing. The Individuals with Disabilities Education Act (IDEA), 2004 identifies 13 education-related disabilities including emotional disturbance (ED). Like all of the other federal definitions it is meant to identify circumstances that must be met in order for the student to be eligible for special education services under the ED category. The federal definition for ED is as follows:

> Emotional disturbance means a condition exhibiting one or more of the following characteristics over a long period of time and to a marked degree that adversely affects a child's educational performance: (A) An inability to learn that cannot be explained by intellectual, sensory, or health factors. (B) An inability to build or maintain satisfactory interpersonal relationships with peers and teachers. (C) Inappropriate types of behavior or feelings under normal circumstances. (D) A general pervasive mood of unhappiness or depression. (E) A tendency to develop physical symptoms or fears associated with personal or school problems. Emotional disturbance includes schizophrenia. The term does not apply to children who are socially maladjusted, unless it is determined that they have an emotional disturbance under paragraph (c)(4)(i) of this section. (Federal Register, 2006, p. 467–56)

This definition is vague. It can be used for almost any child at any time. Also, the outcomes for students labeled with the ED label are some of the worst in all of special education (Knestrict, 2017). For example, "B. *An inability to build or maintain satisfactory personal relationships.*" What constitutes a satisfactory personal relationship? Also the preamble to the definition: "*Emotional disturbance means a condition exhibiting one or more of the following characteristics over a long period of time and to a marked degree that adversely affects a child's educational performance.*"

How long is a "long period of time?" Or "a marked degree?" This vague definition allows the teachers and administrators a tremendous amount of latitude in the educational future of children being considered for this label.

Even the assessment measures used to identify students with this label concentrate on the differences and the deficits of these children being considered. The Behavior Evaluation Scale (BES) (McCarney & Leigh, 1990) is an observational measure used to assist teachers, parents, and staff in identifying students with ED that separates out deficit behaviors as organized by this federal definition. The legitimacy of these measures goes unchallenged by most districts or parents.

These social constructions, ED definition, difference, normality are framed within the context of there being an existing definition of normal. The people in power create the macro-system definition of normal; the hegemonic definition of normal is created through the use of empirical measures, established norms of the group (Baglieri & Knopf, 2004). Those not measuring up become what Foucault (1973) called "the other," outside of the norm and often medicalized, moving from displaying "disturbed behavior" to a pseudo-medicalized label of "disturbed" (Bornstein, 2017).

Once defined and "medicalized," their behavior is systematically modified using methods of ABA that manipulate using rewards and punishments and attempt to externally drive new behaviors determined to be "normal" in the eyes of those in power. This insidious power structure that is created and in use every day in our public schools affects students of color, students from lower socioeconomic status (SES) and boys in general, more dramatically than others. Elevated suspensions and removals for students who are linguistically, racially/ethnically diverse remain elevated for these students. These outcomes are also positively correlated with an increased likelihood of involvement in the juvenile justice system and academic failure (Krezmien, Leone, & Achilles, 2006). The false belief that the IDEA-based labels reflect real pathology fuels beliefs about the inferiority of groups who seem to "have" these impairments in greater proportions. There is no escaping the stigma a label entails. Also, the benefits of special education placement continue to be questionable (Kavale, 1990; Reschly, 1997). The fact that these issues affect, to a dramatic degree, students in underrepresented groups, and that failure to effectively remediate behavioral issues prior to special education placement may result in labeling, which is of questionable benefit, creates an obvious social justice issue. The larger macro-perspective of these issues is problematic. However, as we scope down to a micro-system level the issues become more insidious and difficult to change.

Systemically these issues will not change until teacher education changes. Consistently teacher preparation programs construct behavior management courses from a "within child" perspective. ABA continues to be the choice of technique and philosophical perspective when dealing with behavioral issues in school. The PBIS model, which is derived from an ABA perspective, continues to be the model of choice in most teacher preparation programs and its legitimacy continues to be strengthened via the biased research that is conducted. Last, a critical theory perspective needs to be instilled in our teachers so they can critically look deeper into the reasons models like PBIS are being used. A more proactive model that prepares teachers for the behavioral realities in schools today is needed. A strength-based management perspective is also needed instead of the deficit-driven current model.

School-Wide Frameworks and Foundations

The PBIS model is structured around a three-tiered system of supports. It is often represented as a triangle split into thirds. The bottom third represents a universal system of management and strategies that apply to all students in a given school. Tier two scopes in and applies to the small group of students who are not responding to tier one supports. Tier three is individualized and targeted, identifying individuals not responding to tier one or tier two supports. While the general structure of the model is universally recognized, the specifics of each and the functional rules of each level are not universal and are left to the schools to work out on their own. This lack of an agreed-upon structure leads to some of the shortcomings of the model that have been described in previous chapters. Also, there is a perceived progression that suggests that with each tier, there is an increase in restrictiveness and an increase in external control. This creates a predictable increase in control focus combined with a lack of faith that the student will ever be able to self-mange his/her behavior. There are a few fundamental changes that when made will increase the effectiveness of the model and encourage the development of an internal locus of control and prevent special education placement and identification.

Difference and the Deemphasis of Special Education

A new, more responsive model would operate under the premise of devaluing special education as the primary method of supporting students with behavioral difficulties. Special education is only a viable choice for 3–5% of the school population (Skiba et al., 2006). Because of this percentile data and data indicating the ineffectiveness of special education as a whole this new model prefers to devalue the placement of students into a special education classification and avoid labeling altogether. It has been shown that using specific language can affect the construction of understanding (Firestone & Scholl, 2015; Lupyan & Bergen, 2016). Language used in the new model will deemphasize words and practices that segregate students from one another. Instead of using "interventions" we will use the term "support." Choices will be used instead of the single word "behavior" and the term "difference" will be used as opposed to any special education-related label.

The Continuum at the Classroom Level

The classroom teacher is an intervention specialist. No special education degree is necessary; only the knowledge that if we can successfully engage students in learning we will create an environment where students wish to be and provide them with the skills to intrinsically motivate and monitor their own behavior there would be no need for PBIS. Some advocate for the dismantling of special education as it exists today (Knestrict, 2017). It is the emphasis of the right hand side of the continuum, that is, reactive techniques like bribes and punishments, that creates the externally addicted students we have in schools today. Research supports the notion that engagement decreases inappropriate behaviors (Toldsen et al., 2017) and that feeling a part of a group that values you, or as Charney (1998) describes as the need to "know" and be "known" reduces the need for reactive management strategies, there would be fewer students requiring any tiered interventions. We would certainly begin to decrease the numbers of students being intervened upon down to the 3–5% that the research states as the number of students requiring such restrictive and externally driven techniques. Emphasis of the skills on the left side of the continuum, that is, social skills, rules, rituals, routines, language, affective skill development, engagement, high-interest activities, and community, are the strategies to prevent the necessity of tier two and three behavioral interventions. Unfortunately, the standards-based curriculum and pacing charts prevent the emphasis of developing these skills. They take time. However, they are the crucial elements in developing an internal locus of control and highly developed affectively skilled children.

If we value the development of these skills and this internally driven mindset our approach needs to change. Currently, there is a preponderance of research that values, instead, externally centered models like an ABA-driven PBIS model. A major curricular readjustment is called for, a change that places a greater value on these affectively driven skills and the development of affectively skilled individuals. Continuing to only value the cognitive development and the academic achievement of students is to sell all of our children short. To continue to use reactive models like PBIS and ABA, which emphasize only the product of compliance and high test scores, and not the process of learning how to learn and manage themselves, will only increase the development of students requiring more external control and who continually need to know "what is in it for them?" when demands are made of them in school.

Conclusion and New Begininngs

Autonomy and an internal locus of control are only gained through language, choice, practice, love, acceptance, and guidance from the community. These acquisitions do not happen as a result of a well-structured tier one support that promises treats for desired behaviors. These skills do not appear because of the threat of punishment or negative reinforcers skillfully arranged in timed intervals over an extended period of time. The obediance and compliance that these methods engender will only remain in place if the rewards and threats escalate as fast as the need for these external motivators grows. Internalization and self-management can only develop in individuals who have been given the chance to manage themselves and who see the value of living life within the guidelines developed by the community they thrive within.

"Joy, the feeling of one's own value; being appreciated and loved by others, feeling useful and capable of production are all factors of enormous value to the human soul" (Montessori, 1949, p. 42). I would submit that they are also the essence of learning to manage oneself in a community.

Enagement in learning and the necessary focus required to deeply learn anything is only deepened when the child is able to mange his/her own behavior. No longer struggling to be seen and noticed, no longer feeling less adequate because they don't understand something, they continue to engage because they want to. Knowing they will not be required to move on because a pacing chart tells them they must; they relax and figure it all out. The same is true with behavior. When the child is part of something greater than themsleves (community); when they agree to live the social contract established by the community they have reason to stay and the patience to learn. How different would our world be if we adopted this type of perspective for all students in all schools? If we focused on the depth of learning instead of the breadth of the standards how many more students would succeed? How many more students would be saved from the ravages of special education identification? These things do not develop with the current framework for education and are made even worse by systems like the current PBIS model. Autonomy and an internal locus of control are only developed when the learning community is pulled together to develop into a cohesive and responsive environment— an environment that values each child and teaches them the value of being free, independent, loveable, and capable of learning anything ... deeply.

References

Alberto, P. A., & Troutman, A. C. (2012). *Applied behavior analysis for teachers.* Upper Saddle River, NJ: Pearson Higher Ed.

Annamma, S., Morrison, D., & Jackson, D. (2014). Disproportionality fills in the gaps: Connections between achievement, discipline and special education in the School-to-Prison Pipeline. *Berkeley Review of Education, 5*(1), p. 53–87

Baglieri, S., & Knopf, J. H. (2004). Normalizing difference in inclusive teaching. *Journal of Learning Disabilities, 37*, 525–529.

Berrios, C. D., & Jacobowitz, W. H. (1998). Therapeutic holding: Outcomes of a pilot study. *Journal of Psychosocial Nursing, 36*(8): 36: 14–8.

Björn, P. M., Aro, M. T., Koponen, T. K., Fuchs, L. S., & Fuchs, D. H. (2015). The many faces of special education within RTI frameworks in the United States and Finland. *Learning Disability Quarterly*. E-pub ahead of the print.

Bornstein, J. (2017). Can PBIS build justice rather than merely restore order? In *The school to prison pipeline: The role of culture and discipline in school* (pp. 135–167). Emerald Publishing Limited.

Boulter, L. (2004). Family–school connection and school violence prevention. *The Negro Educational Review, 55*(1), 27–40.

Bredekamp and Copple, (1997).S. Bredekamp, C. Copple (Eds.), Developmentally appropriate practice in early childhood programs (rev. ed.), National Association for the Education of Young Children, Washington, DC (1997).

Brookfield, S. D. (2015). *The skillful teacher.* San Francisco, CA: Jossey-Bass.

Bryk, A. S., and B. L. Schneider . 2002 . *Trust in schools: A core resource for improvement.* New York: Russell Sage.

Charney, R. S. (1998). *Teaching children to care: Management in the responsive classroom.* Greenfield, MA: Northeast Foundation for Children.

Crisis Prevention Institute (2017). *Non-violent crisis intervention training manual.* Crisis Prevention Institute, Milwaukee, Wisconsin.

Comer, J. (2010). The Yale Child Study Center School Development Program. In J. Meece & J. Eccles (Eds.), Handbook on schools, schooling, and human development (pp. 419–433). New York: Routledge.

Covey, S. (1987). *The seven habits of highly effective people.* New York: Simon and Schuster.

Crisis Prevention Institute. (2017). *Non-violent crisis intervention training manual.* Milwaukee, WI: Crisis Prevention Institute.

Csikszentmihalyi, M. (1997b). Flow and education. *NAMTA Journal 22,* (2), 2–35.

Deslandes, R., & Bertrand, R. (2005). Motivation of parent involvement in secondary-level schooling. *The Journal of Educational Research, 98,* 164–175.

Dweck, C., & Rule, M. (2013). *Mindsets: Helping student to fulfill their potential.* Smith College Lecture Series. North Hampton, MA: Smith College.

Federal Register (2006). Statute/Regs Main » Regulations » Part B » Subpart A » Section 300.8 » c » 4 » i: retrieved from: https://sites.ed.gov/idea/regs/b/a/300.8/c/4/i

Firestone, C., & Scholl, B. J. (2015). Cognition does not affect perception: Evaluating the evidence for "top-down" effects. *Behavioral and Brain Sciences,* 1–72, doi Pub View

Foucault, M. (1973). *The birth of the clinic: An archaeology of medical perception* (A. M. Smith, Trans.). New York, NY: Vintage, 1975.

Foucault, M. (2007). The incorporation of the hospital into modern technology. In J. Crampton & S. Elden (Eds.), *Space, knowledge and power: Foucault and geography* (pp. 141–151). Burlington, VT: Ashgate Publishing Company.

Gartrell, D. (2002). Replacing time-out: Part two—Using guidance to maintain an encouraging classroom. *Young Children, 57*(2), 36–43.

Gee, J. P. (1998). What is literacy? In V. Zamel & R. Spack (Eds.), *Negotiating academic literacies: Teaching and learning across languages and cultures* (pp. 51–61). Mahwah, NJ: Erlbaum.

Geller, E. S. (1989). Applied behavioral analysis and social marketing: An integration for environmental preservation. *Journal of Social Issues, 45*(1), 17–36.

Harry, B., & Klingner, J. (2014). *Why are so many minority students in special education?* New York: Teachers College Press.

Joos, M. (1967). The styles of the five clocks. In R. D. Abrhams & R. C. Troike (Eds.), *Language and cultural diversity in American education*. Englewood Cliffs, NJ: Prentice Hall.

Kamii, C. (1989). *Young children continue to reinvent arithmetic*. New York, NY: Teachers College Press.

Kamii, C., & Clark, F. B. (1993). Autonomy: The importance of a scientific theory in education reform. *Learning and Individual Differences, 5*(4), 327–340.

Kavale, K. (1990). 'Differential programming in serving handicapped students'. In: Wang, M. C., Reynolds, M. and Wahlberrg H. J. (Eds) Special Education: Research and Practice. Oxford: Pergamon Press, pp. 35–55.

Knestrict, T. (2006). *Rules, rituals and routines program guide and study guide*. Lake Zurich, IL: Learning Seed Publishing.

Knestrict, T. (2017). *Special education identification of students with emotional disturbance: A social justice analysis and descriptive case study*. Paper presented at the 2018, CARE Conference in Las Vegas Nevada.

Knestrict, T., & Schoensteadt, L. (2005). Social register and behavior. *The Journal of Children in Poverty, 11*(2), 177–186.

Knestrict, T. D. (2015). Deconstructing the positive behavioral support model and replacing it with the neo-Montessori constructivist intervention model or how Montessori changed my cold data driven heart. *Electronic Journal for Inclusive Education, 3*(3), 4.

Kohn, A. (1995). Teaching children to care. Video Series.

Kohn, A. (1999). *Punished by rewards: The trouble with gold stars, incentive plans, A's, praise, and other bribes*. New York: Houghton Mifflin Harcourt.

Krezmien, M. P., Leone, P. E., & Achilles, G. M. (2006). Suspension, race, and disability: Analysis of statewide practices and reporting. *Journal of Emotional and Behavioral Disorders, 14*(4), 217–226.

Lillard, A. (2007). Montessori: The science being the genius. New York: Oxford University Press.

Lupyan, G., & Bergen, B. (2016). How language programs the mind. *Topics in Cognitive Science, 8*(2), 408–424.

McCarney, S. B., & Leigh, J. E. (1990). *Behavior evaluation scale–2*. Columbia, MO: Hawthorne Educational Services.

Montano-Harmon, M. R. (1991, May). Discourse features of Mexican Spanish: Current research in contrastive rhetoric and its implications. *Hispana, 74*(2), 417–425.

Montessori, M. (1948/1973). *To educate the human potential*. Chennai, India: Kalakshetra Publications.

Montessori, M. (1949). *Absorbent mind*. Oxford: ABC-CLIO.

Montessori, M. (1974). *Education for a new world*. Chennai, India: Kalakshetra Press. (Original work published 1946).

Palmer, P. J. (2007). *The courage to teach: Exploring the inner landscape of a teacher's life*. San Francisco, CA: Jossey-Bass Publishers.

Payne R. K. (1996). *A framework for understanding poverty*. Highlands, TX: aha! Process Inc.

Persi, J., & Pasquali, B. (1999). The use of seclusion and physical restraints: Just how consistent are we? *Child and Youth Care Forum, 28*(2), 87–103.

Piaget, J. (1965). *The moral judgement of the child*. New York, NY: Free Press. (Originally published 1932).

Pink, D. H. (2011). *Drive: The surprising truth about what motivates us*. New York: Penguin.

Rao, P. A., & Landa, R. J. (2014). Association between severity of behavioral phenotype and comorbid attention deficit hyperactivity disorder symptoms in children with autism spectrum disorders. *Autism: The International Journal of Research and Practice, 18*, 272–280.

Reschly, D. J. (1997). *Assessment and eligibility determination in the Individuals with Disabilities Education Act of 1997*. IDEA Amendments of, 65–104.

Rimm-Kaufman, S. E., Fan, X., Chiu, Y.-J., & You, W. (2007). The contribution of the responsive classroom approach on children's academic achievement: Results from a three year longitudinal study. *Journal of School Psychology, 45*, 401–421.

Seefeldt, C., Castle, S., & Falconer, R. (2014). *Social studies for the preschool/primary child* (9th ed.). Englewood Cliffs, NJ: Prentice Hall.

Segal, S. P., Bola, J. R., & Watson, M. A. (1996). Race, quality of care, and prescribing practices in the psychiatric emergency room. *Psychiatric Services, 47*, 282–286.

Skiba, R., Simmons, A., Ritter, S., Kohler, K., Henderson, M., & Wu, T. (2006). The context of minority disproportionality: Practitioner perspectives on special education referral. *Teachers College Record, 108*(7), 1424.

Steiner, M. (2016). Freeing up teachers to learn: A case study of teacher autonomy as a tool for reducing educational inequalities in a Montessori school. *FORUM: For Promoting 3–19 Comprehensive Education, 58*, 421–427.

Sunal, C., & Haas, M. (2002). *Social studies for the elementary and middle grades: A constructionist approach*. Boston, MA: Allyn and Bacon.

Thomas, G., & Loxley, T. (2001). *Deconstructing special education and constructing inclusion*. Buckingham: Open University Press.

Toldson, I. A., McGee, T., & Lemmons, B. P. (2017). Reducing suspensions by improving academic engagement among school-age Black males. In D. J. Losen (Ed.), *Closing the school discipline gap: Research for policymakers*. New York, NY: Teachers College Press.

Trawick-Smith, J. (2017). *Early childhood development: A multicultural perspective* (7th ed.). Upper Saddle River, NJ: Merrill/Prentice Hall.

Vygotsky, L. (1978). Interaction between learning and development. *Readings on the Development of Children, 23*(3), 34–41.

Wong, H. K., & Wong, R. T. (2004). *The first days of school*. Mountainview, CA: Wong Publications.

INDEX